Flying against winds of change

Charles Barrett

Para Angola rapidemente e em força! To Angola swiftly and in numbers!

Portuguese authoritarian leader António Oliveira Salazar's address to the nation in 1961 after revolts in Angola, the jewel in the crown of the Empire, came as Salazar still saw a bright future for an empire stretching across Africa to Macau and East Timor in Asia. A Portuguese liner, the *Santa Maria*, was hijacked mid-Atlantic by opponents of the Salazar regime to alert the world to the lack of full democracy in Portugal. The same year saw a failed army coup in Portugal, probably the closest Salazar came to being ousted since taking power in 1932. The attempted putsch was intended to moderate the Portuguese government's attitude to the demands of nationalist movements in its five African territories, Angola, Mozambique, Cape Verde, Guinea-Bissau and Sao Tome. In December 1961 Portugal was further humiliated when Indian forces invaded Goa to liberate the territory that had been under Lisbon's control for over 400 years. Salazar's response to losing Goa was to warn that no more colonies could be lost and that Portugal would take on any independence movements emerging in Angola, Mozambique, Cape Verde, Guinea-Bissau and Sao Tome. Portugal was the second-poorest European state behind Albania but the African colonies had been rebranded as overseas provinces and were probably a security blanket to many Portuguese.

By 1960 the Força Aérea Portuguesa (FAP) had yet to develop any counterinsurgency doctrines based on how aviation had been used in colonial conflicts such as Kenya, Algeria and French Indochina. But in that year FAP Lieutenant Colonel Amadeu Ferreira wrote in a key article that the new types of wars would see air force close air support (CAS) as its primary role. Later the same year WW2 Royal Air Force Free French Ace Colonel Pierre Clostermann, at the Insituto de Altos Estudos Militares (IAEM) staff college in Lisbon, gave Portuguese military commanders an influential lecture on "Aviation in Subversive War" which reflected on the French experience in Algeria.

Clostermann, who had re-enlisted in the Armée de L'Air for a few months in 1956 to fly the Broussard MH 1521 high-wing monoplane on armed reconnaissance missions in Algeria where the independence war was still in progress, told officers from the three branches of Portugal's armed forces that the air force had to work with land and naval forces to win a guerrilla war, but without air power, the counterinsurgency would be lost. France had also learned from its Indochina and Algeria campaigns that airpower did not need a high-tech solution because modern aircraft and their weapons systems did not cope with an austere support environment. Rotary-winged aircraft could also play a key role in future guerrilla wars, Clostermann spoke to Portugal's top brass in Portuguese, which he was fluent in as born in Brazil to diplomat parents. The French aviator had become friendly with Portuguese leader Salazar in the 1950s.

French H-34 gunship in Algeria. I Strange

In its guerrilla war in Algeria against the Front de Libération Nationale (FLN) from 1954 to 1962 France soon replaced fixed-wing aircraft with Sud-Aviation built Sikorsky H-34 and Vertol H-21 to transport quick-reaction commando teams. In 1955 in the Atlas Mountains south of Algiers a quick-thinking helicopter commander Colonel Felix Brunet put two troops with machine guns strapped to the litters of a Bell H-47 to successfully rout FLN fighters, pinning the French down from higher ground. The ad hoc helicopter gunship would be developed into the first helicopter to be armed adequately, the Sikorsky H-19 with a 20mm cannon, two rocket launchers, two .50-calibre machine guns and a 7.5mm machine gun mounted in the cabin.

But the H-19 was underpowered for its new role and only in 1956 with the advent of the Sikorsky H-34 did the French manage to deploy the gunship with the MG 151/20 20mm cannon, two .50-calibre machine guns and batteries of rockets. The gunships, dubbed Pirates, were used to support troop landings and remain on the scene if needed. In Algeria the French developed a coherent doctrine for helicopter use based on one Pirate and six troop transport helicopters. France's development of vertical firepower and manoeuvrability, as well as air transport logistical supremacy in Algeria, meant it beat its guerrilla adversary the FLN on the battlefield. But the FLN won the insurgency on the diplomatic and global public opinion front, so the French authorities were obliged to hand over Algeria to the FLN.

Pierre Clostermann's paper was enthusiastically digested by Portuguese aviators at home and in the farthermost corners of the Empire. His shared experiences in Lisbon helped to either reinforce or refine the FAP's notions of its role in counterinsurgency. The FAP had also looked at British lessons from Malaya and Kenya and other post WW2 insurgencies where airpower had to project over vast areas with terrain and limited resources. The air force would be most effective with decentralised command structure in each theatre with local FAP commanders, often junior officers like lieutenants, responsible for devising missions to monitor and contain insurgent activity. Twin rebellions erupted in northern Angola in 1961 against Portuguese rule that had lasted nearly 500 years. The first came in February when brutally exploited cotton workers in Baixa do Cassange went on strike. A few days later the União das Populaçoës de Angola (UPA), formed in the mid-1950s and led by Holden Roberto, launched deadly attacks in northern Angola.

The UPA was backed by the US, Algeria and Congo-Kinshasa backed the UPA and used mainly weapons from Eastern Europe. Holden Roberto was born and had grown up in the Belgian Congo. On a visit to Angola in 1951 Roberto had witnessed Portuguese officials mistreating an old African man and he later said this incident

Harpoon at BA 9. FAP

had driven him into seeking a career in independence politics, albeit the armed side of things. By May the UPA had taken control of an area nearly the size of mainland Portugal but the FAP was soon involved in the military response to the violence that left 500 Portuguese settlers, mainly farmers, and 20,000 Africans dead in the jewel of the crown of the Portuguese Empire, twice as big as France.

Portugal had anticipated trouble in northern Angola because of unrest in the neighbouring Belgian Congo, which became independent in 1960, and to ensure air defence of the colony, Base Aérea 9 (BA 9, in the capital, Luanda, was identified as the primary air base to build which would be served to the north and east by a number of sector bases, called Aeródromo Base (AB) and forward airfields, called Aeródromo de Manobras (AM). Luanda Airport already served as Angola's main international hub and the new BA 9 would be built opposite the main terminal and share its runway.

Eight Lockheed PV-2 Harpoons and six Nord Noratlas transports, as the new Esquadra 91 (Esq 91), had been deployed to Luanda in 1960 and along with a handful of

Auster D5s light aircraft were the only FAP aircraft available to help Portuguese troops take on the cotton worker and UPA revolts. The FAP converted the PV-2 and its crews from an anti-submarine role to ground attack by removing their turrets but they still boasted six .5 calibre machine guns in the lower nose. The Harpoons could carry 1,365kg of bombs internally and often had six or eight 122mm HVAR rockets on the wings. Portugal had acquired 31 PV-2Cs and three PV-2Ds from the US Navy between 1953 and 1955 under the Mutual Assistance Defence Pact (MAPD).

It took a while for FAP Harpoon crews to adapt to their new role. Flight Lieutenant Carlos Alves flew the first fire-support mission on 9 February 1961 along the Quela-Cunda Ria Baza highway to support ground troops advancing against mutinous cotton workers. Alves released a 100-pound general purpose (GP) bomb at 500 ft with no delay contact fuse and had to return to BA 9 with the left wing and engine damaged by shrapnel. One of the key early missions for the Esq 91 PV-2s was in late April 1961 when two aircraft from Luanda dropped 350-litre napalm bombs on a 2,000-strong UPA mob surrounding a chapel in Mucaba where about 30 settlers had taken refuge. A pair of T-6s also strafed the UPA crowd after the Harpoon napalm drop. Earlier the same day a Dornier DO-27 piloted by Flight Captain Mario Mascarenhas had descended through low cloud over Mucaba to land in the street leading to the chapel to resupply the defenders of the chapel who were down to about 10 rounds of ammunition per3 man. Capitan Mascarenhas dropped ammunition and medicine boxes in front of the chapel, turned his Dornier round and took to the air at full power over the mob that was yelling and running at the aircraft.

As the war progressed in Angola the PV-2s carried a non-standard machine gun configuration with between six to 12 .303, .50 Browning, 7.62 NATO and 12.7mm depending on availability. South African Al Venter was one of the few foreign war reporters allowed to cover Portugal's African conflicts, which were subject to strict censorship by the Salazar government. Venter likened the Portuguese PV-2 multiple machine gun set-up to the US Air Force's AC-47 Spooky gunship, which was used in the Vietnam War to provide suppressing fire. The PV-2's nose-gun firepower would probably at times rival Spooky in terms of the sheer quantity and rate-of-fire of ammunition targeted against insurgents. The FAP would operate nine Harpoons in Angola until 1970 when they were joined by three from Mozambique. Despite perennial maintenance problems with the type they managed a combined average 1,000 missions per year until the end of the Angolan war in 1974 with only two Harpoons lost in combat, a fitting testament to the flying skills of the Esquadra 91 pilots and the hard work of maintenance crews.

Portugal's answer to US Spooky gunship shows its engine powerin Angola. FAP.

FAP Austers and volunteer pilots join war

By the end of the 1950s Portugal realised it would need to replace ageing light aircraft like De Havilland Tiger Moth biplanes, especially in the harsh and often mountainous terrains of Africa. Following an order to the British aircraft manufacturer Auster from the Portuguese government in 1960 a total 167 three-seat Auster D5/160, with 160 hp Lycoming O-320 engines and D5/180 with 180 hp Lycoming O-360 engines were built in the UK and mostly under license at Oficínas Gerais de Material Aeronáutico (OGMA), the main military aviation maintenance centre near Lisbon. The Força Aérea Portuguesa (FAP) had 50 Austers in 1961 and four in Angola at the Negage base which would soon become involved in operations to pacify the cotton plantation rebellion in 1961.

Without a suitable attack aircraft, the FAP employed the Auster to drop army hand grenades to disperse striking cotton workers threatening local Europeans. Flight Sergeant Lemos Carvalhäo, flying serial 3501, had an army officer sat in the co-pilot seat with a box of grenades that had been carefully placed in suitably sized glass jars and the safety pin removed as a makeshift delay fusing, which allowed the relatively slow plane to escape the blast. The Auster attacks over three days killed dozens of rebels and badly injured many more. The Auster's use as a bomber became known as the Malange method after the place it was first used and it would be a few more times during the long insurgency that ended over a decade later. Flight Brigadier Fernando Resende, the FAP commander in Angola, said the Auster hand grenade attacks on the cotton workers had been more effective than the ones by PV-2 BA 9 Harpoons, whose crews were still getting used to ground attack missions.

Civilian pilots in Angolan Aero Clubs in 1961 volunteered to help the Army and FAP in both the cotton-worker uprising and initial UPA guerrilla incursions for medevac, reconnaissance and supply of food, munitions and arms to besieged villages and isolated Portuguese troops in the remote and mountainous region, where road links were rudimentary even before rebel sabotage began. The patriotic, plucky and resourceful civilian pilots from various walks of life knew the mainly mountainous region intimately and often had to land near army columns for protection when returning from missions as darkness fell.

These pilots mainly flew Austers, a few Piper Cubs, and the odd Tiger Moth, and would soon be institutionalised when the Portuguese government created Formações Aéreas Voluntárias (FAV) in May 1962. More voluntary squadrons would be created in Angola and Mozambique, where another colonial war had erupted. FAV pilots often attended briefings with Esquadra 91 Lockheed PV-2 Harpoon crews and the new Esquadra 93 F-84G jet squadron when it began operating later in 1961. The civilian pilots, who were provided with fuel and maintenance facilities, and FAV 201 was the first voluntary squadron formed at BA 9, Luanda.

FAP Auster and FAV pilots. R Duarte.

The pilots were subject to their own disciplinary procedures for offences like flying too low. In June 1961 two voluntary pilots, Albino Leite and Rui Freira, made a forced landing in an Auster after taking supplies to a village besieged by UPA guerrillas. One pilot survived the crash but was shot dead by guerrillas as he tried to escape. Other aviators joined the FAV and probably the most colourful was José Rebelo, aged 69, who purchased his own Piper Cub and resumed his call sign from the Spanish Civil War, Viriato do Ar, when he had flown with the Nationalist air arm in his own Miles Hawk Major.

In principle the Auster D series was highly suited for use in Africa with its metal wing spars, low-flammability long-weathering plastic-based butyrate dope and paint finishes, but Brigadier Fernando Resende, the FAP commander in Angola, thought the Austers too fragile and fickle to be relied on and wanted them replaced as soon as possible with French Broussard MH-1521s and German DO-27s so the Austers could all be transferred to the Aero Clubs and FAVs. The Austers were tricky to land, being very light and sensitive in crosswinds. The relatively small brake pedals were positioned behind the larger rudder pedals instead of being combined into single ones.

Rollout was tricky for inexperienced pilots as the brakes were erratic and only experienced aviators fully mastered the plane's idiosyncrasies. Another major design flaw on the British aircraft was having the flap lever on the opposite side of the cockpit to the throttle, meaning pilots had to switch hands at critical moments of approach and landing. But despite Brigadier Resende's reservations about the Auster the D5/160 and D5/180 the British-designed planes continued to be flown by both the FAP and FAV volunteer squadrons with around 30 being used for liaison, reconnaissance and supply missions until 1974 when the Angolan war ended.

On Sundays the FAV voluntary pilots often ferried troops from remote bases to larger towns to go to Mass. The remaining fatal Auster crashes were FAP serial 3524 in September 1964 with one killed; FAV civil registration CR-LEA in February 1965 with one dead; FAV civil registration CR-LEV at Onzo in January 1966 with one fatality.6 In April 1971 FAP serial 3522 with a FAV pilot crashed killing one and in March 1973 FAP serial 3334 with a FAV pilot was lost with one death. Auster, named after the Roman god for the south wind, was taken over by Beagle Aircraft in September 1960 and the D5/180 became the Beagle Huskey.

Beagle attempted to find customers, particularly overseas, for the aircraft after the Portuguese contract which had been a shot in the arm for the British company with the final aircraft delivered in January 1962. Beagle built another D5/180 as a demonstrator in a bid to get further sales and G-ASBV made its first flight in July 1962. Beagle sales and test pilot Vyrell Mitchel flew the aircraft across the Channel for demonstrations with the Belgian Army but the D5 overturned on landing at a wooded clearing strip near Antwerp. The accident was attributed to inefficiency of the braking system and wheels that were too small.

Another problem identified by the potential Belgium customers was the positioning of the flap control lever on the side of the cockpit which had made it virtually impossible for the pilot to exit the crashed demonstrator. A central roof-mounted flap lever was subsequently fitted to the D5, as well as hydraulic brakes, but the Belgian military opted for a rival plane. Beagle made only 15 Huskys before production was stopped in 1967. Each aircraft was made to customer specifications so manufacture was uneconomic with each plane costing £6,045, nearly a third more than the UK market price.

In May a few more T-6Gs armed with 7.5mm machine guns, 37mm rocket pods and 100 kgs of bombs arrived in the region to provide ground support to troops in actions that alleviated some enemy pressure on the local populations. Portugal would eventually acquire 56 T-6Gs from the US under the Mutual Defence Assistance Program and another 200, including Canadian Car and Foundry-built Harvards, from surplus stocks in France, West Germany, South Africa and the UK.

The lumbering and unarmored T-6G was ironically dubbed the "F-110", meaning 110kt at takeoff, 110kt in the cruise and 110kt on landing. The former trainer was first produced in 1939 and its stalling speed was dangerously close to its bomb-dropping one. However, its slow speed made it an accurate machine gun and rocket platform and

T-6 or 'F-110' over Angola. FAP

with careful fuel management the T-6G could stay in the skies for around four hours. But it required two to three minutes to make a strafing pass and almost twice as long for a bombing run so consequently suffered more battle damage per sortie than any other FAP type and had the highest fatality rate from operational losses and accidents.

In the same month the FAP took delivery of more Dornier DO-27s in Angola which was a welcome development for the FAP because the reconnaissance, liaison, resupply and forward air control. The Dornier was the first aircraft manufactured in West Germany after WW2 and had a minimum flying speed of 24 knots, with full flaps applied, knots and 460 feet takeoff run.

The short-takeoff machine was extremely well adapted to rudimentary airfields and was used for reconnaissance, transport of troops and cargo as well as medevac. It was rugged and had a generous cargo capacity and could also fly at night. Portugal eventually acquired 150 DO-27s and the utility aircraft could also be fitted with 37mm rocket pods on each wing, although this kind of mission was normally allocated to the T6. However, the FAP was looking for an aircraft with altogether more firepower to help restore order in northern Angola because the aged Harpoons had maintenance issues and weren't always ready for action.

Thunder over Angola

In the early 1960s the Salazar government had begun looking for a bomber that could be used in the close-support role and approached European allies including its oldest ally dating from 1386, England, which offered six ex-RAF Canberra B Mk 2s for a combined £500,000. But in 1962 the Conservative government of Harold Macmillan had warned Lisbon the Canberras could not be sent to the African colonies and must remain at home for use in Portugal's NATO role and training. Portugal would make another attempt to buy Canberras but eventually realised the British jet, primarily designed for high altitudes and with large wings, was not suited for the COIN role and would also be costly to maintain in the African theatre. The Portuguese would also learn that Rhodesia had been sold the same British bombers for significantly less, which proved to be the last straw in the deal.

The FAP had been supplied with 120 Republic F-84Gs in 1953 on the Mutual Defence Assistance Program (MDAP) and the Thunderjets had been replaced by Sabre F-86Fs in 1958 as Portugal's main aerial combat jet. Coming into service in 1951 the F-84G was the final version of the Thunderjet with a framed canopy that was retrofitted to earlier bubble canopy machines that had proved insufficiently robust. The F-84G had been built as the USAF's first nuclear bomber to carry a 544 kg tactical weapon, and the sturdy jet with a 1,814 kg maximum ordinance was still seen as highly useful by the FAP for some roles like delivering heavy fire support, particularly in a permissive environment with no appreciable AAA threat. The Thunderjet featured an Allison J35 turbojet with 2,540 kgp/5,600 lb thrust, which were in dire need of replacement on the FAP machines, especially if the decade-old jets were going to be the linchpin of fire-support missions in Angola.

Portugal bought its F-84Gs outright at the equivalent of $ 208,995 per unit which ended MDAP restrictions and allow the jets to be sent to Africa because they were categorised as NATO surplus. Portugal was fortunate to acquire a large supply of J-35s with zero hours operation from a private US firm, without objections from the American authorities, and a dozen F-84Gs had arrived in Luanda by June 1961 in separate sea shipments to form the new Esquadra 93, *Os Magníficos*, or Magnificent Ones. Esq 91 would lose its first Harpoon on June 8 when 4620 crashed on a bombing mission in northern Angola, killing its two pilots and three other aircrew.

F-84G at BA9. FAP

The first flight of the Esquadra 93 F-84Gs was on 17 August when the new unit's commander, Flight Major Costa Gomes, and his wingman overflew central Luanda and its South Atlantic beaches to announce the arrival of the jets that would soon be in action against UPA fighters who had consolidated their grip on northern Angola over an area almost the size of Portugal. The Portuguese Army was beginning to regain control of some part of northern Angola several offences and the first airborne assault in Portuguese military history on 11 August when a flight of FAP C-54s dropped paratroopers in Operation Nema to retake the town of Quipedro.

A Dornier Do-27 used smoke rockets to mark the landing zone (LZ) 30 minutes before the jump and Harpoons and T6s covered the area with withering fire to protect the troops from any UPA ambush. A Do-27 coordinated the operation which successfully killed or captured dozens of insurgents. The FAP would not create a helicopter squadron for another year or two at BA 9 so the C-54s and Noratlas were used for troop insertion in the meantime in operations to dislodge UPA groups.

PV-2s and T6Gs performed valiantly to attack UPA strongholds in two districts to restore control to Portuguese ground forces while the FAP continued the monitor guerrilla movements, often using reports from FAV volunteer pilots in fragile Austers in preparation for deployment of the Thunderjet's more potent firepower.

The FAP high command in Angola had identified 500 lb bombs and 350 litre napalm canisters as being the weapons that would be most needed to dislodge UPA fighters from their new mountaintop strongholds and provide close-air support for ground troops on anti-guerilla sweeps. Despite Esquadra 93's late arrival to the Angolan conflict its Thunderjets had carried out 43 missions against UPA positions in August with 32 of these being solo attacks, called *destruição localizada* (DLOC).

The baptism of fire for the new jets was on 25 August when a formation of Thunderjets provided close air support for elite Paras retaking Canda. On 19 September Os Magnificos attacked Scandica in another support of a Para drop but the jets were still armed with totally inadequate 100 lb bombs because of a shortage of larger ones at BA 9. The 350-litre napalm bombs were also in short supply and on 10 September the FAP commander in Luanda notified Lisbon that the base only had 110 350-litre napalm canisters and 90 500 lb bombs, sufficient for around 15 days of F-84G and Harpoon operations against the UPA.

Later the same month Esquadra 93 participated in an operation to recover the town of Beira Baixa with pilots making pinpoint drops of napalm canisters less than 300 metres from columns of Portuguese troops because of a lack of 500-pound bombs or 2.7-inch rockets. On 10 October the Thunderjets took part in a joint operation with Harpoons to dislodge insurgents from Serra da Canaga, a huge elevated plateau obscured by dense foliage. Even in the early stages of its Angolan war Portugal's use of napalm was strictly restricted to operations where bombs or rockets could not be used and the colony's terrain was normally not suitable for napalm use. But the FAP did allow limited napalm in its other African wars with an average of 12.6 tonnes per month dropped in Guinea and 4.2 tonnes in Mozambique.

At least one of the Esquadra 93 jets had been fitted with a reconnaissance camera in one of its wingtip tanks and Flight Lieutenant Alcico Roque proved to be the most successful at finding guerrilla camps in the undulating terrain. One of Roque's low-level photos showed the UPA headquarters and the plan was for four F-84s to bomb from altitude in a steep angle to place two 750-pound bombs with precision.

Esq 93 pilots by Thunderjet with napalm canisters. F Moutinho (second from left standing)

Three Harpoons would then in sequence drop salvos of 18 200-pound bombs. One of the Thunderjet pilots, Flight Lieutenant António Dias, in FAP serial 5180, developed target fixation in his bombing run and failed to exit successfully. The UPA stronghold was successfully destroyed in the two-wave attack but the loss of the youthful officer was keenly felt by all at BA 9.

1962 another 13 F-84s arrived reinforcing Esquadra 93 to 25 jets and the squadron flew over 2,000 armed reconnaissance and mainly close support missions yearly for the first four years of the deployment. The jet squadron's average monthly use of 350-pound bombs and 350-litre napalm canisters was around 50 in this period with about 200 2.75inch rockets with an average of 86,000 .5 calibre rounds for the F-84's six Browning machine guns, which were armed for each mission.

A sporadic mission for the Esquadra 93 pilots they'd had zero training for, and a stern test of their low-level precision, was as a newspaper delivery to troops in the isolated Cabinda enclave. Magazines and newspaper were bundled with cord and placed between the jet's belly and large air brake when being retracted at BA 9 in Luanda. A pair of F-84s armed only with machine guns was often sent to patrol Cabinda and the Congolese border so a jet would approach an army base at around 150 ft and time the opening of the hydraulic air brakes to deliver the eagerly awaited cargo. The Thunderjets would also fly in pairs on these missions to Cabinda so the second jet would usually manage to deliver to another army base. Because BA 9 was also Angola's main international airport it was easy for the FAP personnel to acquire surplus publications from patriotic newsstands for the Cabinda newspaper drops.

In June 1962 Esquadra 93 had its second fatality when F-84G serial 5177 with Flight Sergeant António Carneiro was lost on a combat mission in northern Angola. In June 1964 Flight Lieutenant Francisco Navarro's Thunderjet 5128 crashed in the sea off Luanda at night on approach to BA9 due to spatial disorientation of the pilot and in early 1965 F-84G serial 5128 flown by Flight Capitan Luis Simões was lost in combat in northern Angola. In September 1965 another joint Harpoon and Thunderjet operation was launched to destroy UPA bases in the Serra de Uige mountains with bombing so intense the BA9 arsenal had only two days of munitions.

In late 1966 another Angolan independence group, the Movimento Popular de Libertaçao de Angola (MPLA), formed in 1956 by the Angolan Communist Party and led by Agostinho Neto, began another campaign in remote eastern Angola near the Zambian border. The MPLA had participated in an earlier rebellion against Portugal in Luanda in 1961. The MPLA was supported by the Soviet Union and Cuba, which trained most of its fighters and supplied Russian weapons. Esquadra 93 was instructed to send a pair of Thunderjets in a show of force against the MPLA, which had started to seek support from local villagers.

One of the squadron's most experienced pilots, Flight Captain Fernando Moutinho, was chosen to lead the mission which would land at AB 4, Henrique de Carvalho, after the 1,000 km flight and fly several more of the psychological operations over a few days and check for insurgent activity. As Esquadra 93 had to date only operated in northern Angola on anti-UPA missions it had no maps of eastern Angola but Captain Moutinho and his wingman were supplied with ones of US origin which were to give them some navigational headaches in reaching AB 4. Departing BA 9 in Luanda at about 16.00 on December 25, 1966, the two F-84Gs climbed to 20,000 ft and followed the course the pilots had plotted on the new maps to reach Henrique de Carvalho, whose radio beacon was out of action. The F-84Gs descended through cloud to 2,000 ft about 2 miles west of AB 4 but realised they were lost as there was no sign of the airfield.

The pilots scanned the barren terrain for landmarks and spotted the name of a village painted on the roof of a building, the custom in most countries at the time, and realised they were 50 miles from AB 4. The Thunderjets then flew towards the base, contacting the tower, and overflew it before proceeding west for about 30 miles to the Zambian border where the MPLA activity had been reported. As it was getting dark the Thunderjets requested AB 4 to turn on its landing lights and Moutinho and his wingman finally landed after three hours in flight with around 10 minutes of fuel in their tanks.

Over the coming three days the two F-84Gs overflew the suspected MPLA positions several times without spotting any enemy activity before returning to Luanda. After these navigational problems on Esq 93's first mission to eastern Angola the FAP began making its own maps based on photo reconnaissance from DC-3 and Do-27 flights over the region. In September 1967 the

MPLA group in eastern Angola. MSF.

squadron lost another Thunderjet when Flight Lieutenant Manuel Silva crashed on a combat mission. The fifth and final Thunderjet loss for Esquadra 93 was in April 1969 when Capitan António Abrantes in 5213 collided with 5130 near Luanda. One of the tip tanks on Abrantes' machine ignited and the Thunderjet became a fireball. The other jet did not catch fire and managed to land at BA 9.

From 1968 to 1972 the F-84Gs flew around 200 combat missions per year and during the war the original tip tanks on the Thunderjets were replaced in field with larger Fletcher-style ones from the FAP T-33s. Flight Capitan Vitor Silva was the last Esquadra 93 pilot to fly the F-84G in 1973 on an armed reconnaissance mission from BA 9. The jet had become increasingly expensive to maintain and was gradually replaced in Esquadra 93 by even older Douglas B-26 Invaders. One of the most interesting stories on service careers of Portuguese military aircraft is the one concerning the Douglas B-26 Invader and particularly the unorthodox way it entered the FAP inventory. By 1965 the FAP needed to replace its ageing bomber fleet being used in Africa for close support such as PV-2 Harpoons but realised the task would be difficult because of a UN embargo on arms sales to Portugal.

Thunderjet being towed at BA9 with Noratlas and Harpoons in background. F Moutinho

Portugal gets B-26 bombers - eventually

Portugal used a Swiss arms dealer to reach an agreement with Aero Associates of Tucson, Arizona, to obtain 20 Invaders that would be refurbished by Hamilton Aircraft in the same city with the last aircraft to be delivered to Portugal by January 1996. Spare parts and accessories were included in the deal that was worth USD 450,000. Aero Associates was owned by Gregory Board, a World War 2 fighter veteran, who hired ex-RAF pilot John Hawke to ferry the B-26s to Portugal at USD 3,000 per flight but the British pilot had to pay all expenses including fuel and commercial airline tickets back to the US so he averaged around USD 700 per trip.

Board and Hawke had met in 1963 in the UK during filming for *633 Squadron* where both flew Mosquitos. In May 1965 Hawke took off from Tucson with the first B-26 and flew to Rochester, New York, to spend a night in a hotel and pick up additional equipment. The next day he flew to Newfoundland and cleared Canadian customs and continued on towards Santa Maria in the Portuguese Azores Islands before completing the final leg to Tancos, an FAP base near Lisbon, where he was met by enthusiastic Portuguese officials and whisked by car to nearby Lisbon Airport to catch the next available flight to America.

On his second B-26 ferry flight Hawke ran into bad weather near Washington and his radio and compass malfunctioned so he decided to put in at Washington National Airport. As he made his approach at around 1,000 ft he unknowingly flew directly over the White House but when questioned by police gave the codeword "sparrow" which secured his immediate release. Hawke was sternly told that the offence of breaching White House airspace usually carried a USD 1,000 fine. John Hawke managed to deliver seven B-26s to Portugal when he was detained in America in September 1965 when trying to collect parts including a bomb sights and machine gun accessories for the Invaders in a C-46. One C-46 flight with Invader spares for Portugal had already been made by Gregory Board.

Hawke was put on trial for breaking the US Munitions Control Act along with another pilot, Henri Marie François de Marin de Montmarin, a debonair French count who had won the Légion d'honneur as a Free French fighter pilot in World War 2 and was accused of being the European intermediary in the affair. Gregory Board was also indicted but managed to flee to Jamaica. Hawke told the trial he had flown B-26s to Portugal for use in Africa and the operation was arranged by the US State Department and CIA and called Operation Sparrow. Both Hawke and de Montmarin were acquitted by the court in Buffalo, New York.

Invader at OGMA. FAP.

The proceedings were described as a light-hearted affair by court reporters and the judge had even permitted Hawke to ferry a plane to France and back over a weekend. After John Hawke's American trials and tribulations and partial delivery of the 20 B-26s by September 1965 the FAP was the proud owner of seven complete Invaders with provisions for armament but only the bombing and gun electrical circuits, a few spares from the single C-46 delivery but no armament. The serials 7101 to 7107 were issued to the FAP B-26, repeating some given in 1952 to the FAP's Grumman SA-16 Albatross.

In late 1966 it was decided to equip the FAP bombers with six .50 Browning M2 machine guns in the nose, apart from serial 7102 which had M2s under the wings because of its plexiglass nose. In the bomb bays two hard points would be installed for 50 or 200 kg bombs and equipment to release 15 KG bombs and each wing would have two hard points for 4 2.5" rockets, or 18 37mm rockets. Due to a lack of spares for the B-26s until 1970 operational testing was only undertaken on 7101, with dual controls, in September 1967 and 7106 in July 1969 and 7107 in September 1970. In 1970 these three Invaders were sent to Guinea-Bissau, where the FAP was engaged in another guerrilla war, as a tropical testing detachment.

In the meantime the FAP attempted to source more spares for its Invader fleet which finally came from France in 1970 which allowed the complete refurbishment of the aircraft that started in early 1971 at Oficínas Gerais de Material Aeronáutico (OGMA), with the aircraft completely stripped down, wing-spars reinforced and armaments installed. By November 1971 the B-26s had all been refurbished except 7104, which was scrapped due to heavy corrosion and donated to the Museu do Ar at Sintra. During 1973 the six B-26s were a familiar sight around Lisbon as they made more test flights from OGMA around the capital and to the Azores, Madeira and the Spanish Canary Islands. In 1973 the remaining six Invaders were finally sent to replace Esquadra 93's ageing F-84Gs which is a rare case of piston-engined aircraft replacing jets in an operational bomber squadron.

Pilots in Angola appreciated the B-26's armour around the cockpit as well as the thick Plexiglass windscreens that gave better protection against ground fire as unless a round hit the Plexiglass at 90 degrees the material would deflect it. The first missions for the Invaders were in support of Puma and Alouette III troop insertions as well as designated bombing and armed reconnaissance. The six Invaders flew a combined 653 hours in 1973, but the US bomber was never fully integrated into FAP operations and remained a specialist assignment for pilots, who were usually expected to fly several types of aircraft. The B-26s were viewed by many as FAP stepchildren and all six were left in Angola in 1975 when Portugal relinquished control of the colony. The July 1966 edition of *FlyPast* carried a photo of four of them taken 50 km south of Luanda where the remains of 7102, 7103, 7106 and 7105 could be seen.

Ex-FAP B-26 near Luanda. R Wisely

Invader at OGMA after conversion. 'Red devils' sqd marking.
FAP

B-26 with anti-missile paint at BA9. FAP

FAP develops word's first Alouette gunship and gets brand new Pumas

Portugal began creating a helicopter force in 1958 with the purchase of seven SA-318C Alouette II and six of these machines were sent to Angola in 1962. The FAP acquired 12 SA-316 Alouette III helicopters in June 1963 that formed the new Esquadra 94, *Moscas*, or flies, at BA 9. Portugal was the first export customer for the Alouette 3, also designed as a civil utility machine but proving to be a magnificent military machine using jet fuel but able to operate on diesel and petrol in emergencies on short flights. It could absorb significant amounts of small-arms fire and even hits from RPGs.

The Alouette 3 was basically an enlarged and more powerful Alouette II with an Artouste IIB turboshaft engine of 870/550 SHP and a reinforced transmission system. In the first years of its Angolan guerrilla war the FAP had experienced problems depositing troops by parachute due to inherent variables and vulnerabilities. Wind was a potent factor that could injure troops on landing or even make them miss the LZ. But the helicopter could drop a force swiftly next to a target for its easy capture or destruction. A one-minute flight in a helicopter was equivalent to an hour on foot in the jungle.

Portuguese military chiefs had paid close attention to France's guerrilla war in Algeria from 1954 to 1962 where Sikorsky H-34 helicopters with a MG-151 20mm cannon and other machine guns was used as a gunship covering troop landings by six transport helicopters. The FAP took several years to fully develop its Alouette III gunship assisted by Sud Aviation technicians. Initially hand-held AR-10 automatic rifles, used by Portuguese troops, were tried but found to have too little firepower. A 12-gauge shotgun with buckshot cartridges had some success but something altogether more potent was needed to protect the LZs from guerrilla attention. The MG-42 (7.62mm) light machine gun proved difficult to handle and the movement of the helicopter meant it couldn't be held on target.

In 1964 the F-84G's Browning M3 (.50 calibre) were tried in a side-by-side configuration in the left door of the Alouette III slaved to a target visor from a T-6G. The dual M3 mount worked partially giving more robust fire support but was cumbersome with the extra weight and ammunition. By early 1965 the French Matra MG-151 20mm cannon, mounted on floor fittings aiming out of port rear windows, was found to be the perfect solution with its low recoil and 700 rounds per minute firing rate, which could be adjusted downwards to 350. High explosive incendiary (HIE) rounds were the most effective against guerrillas and gunners would be trained to look for hard rocks or hard ground to maximise shrapnel damage.

Esq 94 Al 3 at BA9. Luanda Airport tower in background. F Cruz

The HIE round was not effective if fired onto soft ground which absorbed their explosive effect or made the inertia fuses fail to decelerate sufficiently to ignite. For deflection shooting the MG-151 had a Collimateur reflector gun sight calibrated for 90 degrees to the fore and aft axis from 800 ft at 65 knots and good gunners could fire accurately from lower heights and some preferred 600 ft. But often the Alouette III gunship would be used at ranges of as little as 100ft at treetop level when insurgents were encountered in clearings after stealthy approaches.

A higher percentage of guerrillas was probably killed or wounded by HEI fire from the Alouette gunships than by the weapons of Portuguese troops in the Angolan theatre. The MG-151 could be fed with 200 or 400-round boxes. HEI rounds were expensive so gunners often used bursts of 3 rounds or less but the MG-15, the pilot and gunner plus two ammunition boxes and a 450 litre jet fuel load made the Alouette gunship version heavy and its centre of gravity shifted forward and was often difficult to fly so only experienced FAP pilots got to fly them.

The lead pilot in the five -helicopter flight was the key to inserting the 20-man combat group and was usually qualified in both fixed-wing aircraft and helicopters. He would often get to know the local theatre at low level in a Dornier DO-27 marking suitable helicopter landing sites for future operations. Approach routes to the landing sites would also be marked and the sites were often chosen for suitable terrain to mask the sound of five noisy helicopters from insurgents.

Troops rehearsed operations until ready to go into action and the combat group would be kept on standby at BA 9, Luanda, until the operation was imminent when it would move to an airfield nearer the area of anticipated operations. The five helicopters and the troops would wait a number of days before launching the mission, which depended on total surprise, with reconnaissance of the area kept to a minimum. The four Alouette III troop carriers and gunship, which FAP personnel in Angola dubbed the *heli-canão*, would fly to the LZ on a nap-of-the-earth approach with the gunship circling the area before landing the troops and using its MG-151 for suppressing fire if needed. Often a DO-27 would provide extra fire support with its 18 37mm rockets carried in canisters on each wing.

The Dornier's rockets would also be used for smoke marking LZs or insurgent sites. The four troop carriers would loiter nearby because often the action would conclude away from the LZ. The 20-man team and its helicopters would normally stay in the field for the rest of the day, coordinating with ground troops to kill or capture the guerrillas. Some combat units had sufficient field support in fuel, ammunition and maintenance to remain in the field for several days and undertake operations for three to four days before retiring to Luanda to rest for a few days. Occasionally two 20-man assault teams comprising eight transport helicopters and two gunships would be used by the FAP but care was always taken not to insert a troops into an untenable spot where they would be overrun by a larger band of guerillas.

Use of the FAP Alouette III gunships was usually carefully controlled to avoid collateral damage to civilians from indiscriminate use of the MG-151 with assault operations nearly always undertaken away from populated areas. The first large helicopter operation took place in northern Angola in March 1965 involving 2,000 troops and eight Esquadra 94 Alouette IIIs, including two gunships, staging from Santa Eulalia. In August 1966 a third insurgent group, União Nacional para a Independência Total de Angola (UNITA) entered the fight against Portuguese colonial rule and Esquadra 94 Alouette IIIs supported army units pursuing the new guerrilla force for several weeks.

UNITA leader Jonas Savimbi had broken away from the UPA, which had become the Frente Nacional de Libertação de Angola (FNLA). UNITA garnered open support from China, South Africa and covertly from the US via the CIA.

From 1967 to 1970 Esquadra 94 undertook around 300 assault operations yearly, mainly using the four Alouette III troop transports covered by a gunship against the MPLA, UNITA and the UPA/FNLA in northern and eastern Angola until 1970 when the squadron received six Sud-Aviation SA 330S Puma helicopters that could carry 15 fully equipped troops. The Portuguese Puma was a SA 330C modified at

Puma and Paras in northern Angola.
FAP

OGMA with a composite main rotor and two 1,700shp Turbomeca Makila I turboshafts. Some of the helicopter assault operations by Esquadra 94 had been hampered by maintenance problems with the Alouette IIIs, most of which had been operating in Angola's semi-tropical climate and annual rainy season from October to March for eight years.

To help the army claw back some advantage against the three separate insurgencies, particularly the MPLA's Eastern front, tactics changed with the arrival of the Puma to two Puma troop carriers escorted by two Alouette 3 gunships. But the smaller 20-man assault team in four Alouette IIIs covered by a gunship was still used or even combined with a two-Puma flight plus its escorts for the LZ approach and covering.

From 1971 to 1974, the end of the war, Esquadra 94 ramped up its annual assault missions to over 1,000 and 1972 was the peak Alouette deployment in Angola with 37 machines, although some of these South African helicopters given to Portugal to create Esquadra 402, *Saltimbancos*, or traveling entertainers. The South African Alouette IIIs carried no national markings or serials and became known as the black block of helicopter serials to protect the secrecy of increasingly close military ties between Lisbon and Pretoria.

In 1969 Alouette 3s were used in a new tactic of air-ground cooperation on the Eastern Front against MPLA fighters in the first Operation Sirocco, named after the hot dessert wind in that region, which would last the entire dry season for the next three years. The initial Sirocco comprised four Alouette 3s and a Do-27 and elite troops formed hunting teams against suspected or actual MPLA positions. Follow-up operations *Raio* and *Bizarra* in the region had even more success against the MPLA and by October 1973 some 121 fighters had been killed, of whom seven were senior MPLA officials, and around 150 taken prisoner. Senior MPLA official Daniel Chipenda said after the war that the guerrillas had faced a crisis from 1972 after losing control of most of the population in the east of the county, where the Portuguese Army had established protected villages.

Esquadra 94 lost nine Alouette III during the Angolan conflict. Serial 9259 at Luanda in December 1965 with structural failure killing one, 9251 at Luanda in January 1966 killing six and 9292 in May 1968 in Canzundo killing two. In March 1969 serial 9319 crashed into a tree during a night pursuit of an unidentified aircraft. In June 1969 serial 9321 crashed in Quibaxe killing four and in May 1972 serial 9347 crashed in Motumbo killing two after tail rotor failure. In January 1973 9372 was lost in combat with pilot killed and the gunner landing aircraft. In March 1974 9255 was lost in Cagombe killing five. In June 1974 9369 crashed in the Serra do Muabi killing two.

FAP PIper Cub and other aircraft destroyed at Tancos. Publico

Esquadra 94 lost none of its six Pumas in the Angolan war but one was destroyed by Portuguese citizens in Lisbon before it got a chance to be used against Angolan insurgents. In 1971 members of *Acção Revolucianaria Armada* (ARA), the armed wing of the outlawed Partido Comunista Português (PCP), broke into BA 3 at Tancos, near Lisbon, with the intention of destroying FAP aircraft and helicopters bound for Africa. FAP Puma 9507 was destroyed by explosives in the ARA raid along with four Alouette IIIs, three Dornier DO-27s, an Auster and four Piper Cubs. One of the saboteurs, Ângelo de Sousa, was a trainee helicopter pilot and knew the Tancos base well and which hangar to attack. In 1968 Portugal's long-time government chief António Salazar, after becoming ill after a fall from in his deckchair, was replaced as Portuguese leader by his anointed successor, Marcelo Caetano, who ruled until April 25 1974 when he was deposed in a coup led by war-weary junior army officers.

End of Salazar-Caetano era triggers uncertainty in Angola

Hostilities in Portugal's three African colonies largely ceased but the situation on the ground in Angola became confused as the MPLA, UNITA and FNLA tried to consolidate the respective areas they had taken control and some bitter fighting still carried on, particularly between the MPLA and FNLA. Additionally, with an uncertain future as Angola moved inexorably towards being an independent state, Portuguese settlers began to move towards towns and cities, particularly Luanda in case a swift repatriation to Portugal by air was decided in Lisbon. The FAP had had no jet bombers in Angola since Esq 93's ageing Thunderjets had been retired at the end of 1972 so it was decided to deploy some Fiat G 91s from Mozambique to Luanda in November 1974.

Fiat from Jaguars Squadron. I Strange

Fiats from Esquadra 502 Jaguares, Jaguars and Esquadra 702 Escorpiões Scorpions, were disassembled and sent by air freight from Nacala to Luanda. The Fiat G 91 R/4 used by the FAP was identical to the R/1 version used by the Italian Air Force with an additional two underwing hardpoints and the same avionics as the Luftwaffe's R/3 version. The Portuguese Fiats had a maximum bomb load of 680 kg comprising two 340 kg bombs on the wing root stations. They could also carry eight SNEB 70mm rockets on the outboard stations or four 50 kg bombs in place of the rockets. The most common weapons configuration was four outboard 50 kg bombs with two 200 kg ones on the inner stations. Two 320 litre external fuel tanks could be carried on the root station and the G.91 was also armed with four 0.5-calibre machine guns with 300 rounds apiece. The Fiat detachment was based at BA 9 in Luanda until October 1975 and mainly undertook reconnaissance missions to monitor movements by MPLA, UNITA and FNLA fighters. The G-91s also operated from AB 3 Negage, AB 95 Cabinda and some smaller airstrips to provide top cover to army columns that were in turn escorting vehicles of Portuguese settlers towards Luanda. The Fiat jets were designed to operate from smaller airfields, including unimproved ones, so was useful for counterinsurgency work. The Angola-based Fiats were only obliged to use their weapons once in November 1974 against independence fighters from the Frente para a Libertação do Enclave de Cabinda (FLEC) who had taken control of part of the Cabinda enclave.

In 1975 as Angola headed towards its independence Portugal and some NATO allies, as well as Warsaw Pact states like East Germany and the USSR, created a free air bridge with mainly civil and some military planes between Luanda and Lisbon to permit Portuguese and other nationalities to leave. Portuguese state airline TAP introduced a Boeing-747 Jumbo on the route in May, which was the peak month. By 4 October some 27,600 Portuguese had left the colony for Portugal and the free flights to Lisbon were creased from the end of October as Angolan independence loomed on 11 November, the final date for Portuguese troops to leave under the Alvor Accord between the MPLA, UNITA, the FNLA and the Lisbon government. There were also some direct flights from Luanda to Porto because about a third of the Angolan settlers were originally from impoverished regions of northern Portugal. Like Tras os Montes. Around 500,000 Portuguese settlers, mainly from Angola and Mozambique, came back to Portugal in 1975 and were given the status of *retorandos*, or returnees, by the Lisbon government which was facing a range of social and economic woes in the wake of the bloodless 1974 army rebellion.

On 2 November 1975 Flight Captain Fernando Moutinho received his final orders in his nine-year posting to Angola to bring Noratlas 6415 from BA 9 in Luanda to Lisbon as the clock ticked down to the 11 November independence of the colony. BA 9 was virtually deserted and in something of a sorry state and Moutinho went to the squadron bar for a final visit. He'd arrived there in 1966 to join Esquada 93 on F-84G Thunderjets and been transferred to FAP's transport squadron in 1968 where he was to clock up over 4,000 hours on the Noratlas. Virtually the only object left in the mess was a framed picture on the wall of *Nossa Senhora do Ar*, Our Lady of the Air, the patron saint of Portuguese airmen. Beneath

BA 9-based Our Lady of Air picture. F Moutinho

the photo somebody had written in ink, *Perdoai-lhes porque eles não sabem o que fazem* – forgive them because they didn't know what they were doing. Moutinho took the relatively small picture of the pilots' good luck charm that many airmen would briefly touch before going on combat missions and still has it in his bedroom in Portugal.

Two weeks previously Moutinho had been instructed to hand over AB 4 at Henrique de Carvalho to the MPLA, to whom the outgoing Portuguese colonial administration had appeared to favour over the rival UNITA and FNLA forces, which were being driven out of the main cities including Luanda by the MPLA. Around 70 FNLA guerrillas were hiding in a hangar at AB4, which had to be transferred to the MPLA that day, so Moutinho and the crew of his Noratlas would have to devise a way of getting the FNLA soldiers out of the hangar at AB 4 as the two Angolan guerrilla armies had become bitter enemies over many years it was highly likely that the FNLA soldiers would have faced summary execution.

The MPLA contingent arrived at AB4 in vehicles and Capt. Moutinho invited then to the officers' mess and kept them taking as the other members of his crew quickly got the FNLA group to hide in trunks and large suitcases in the hold of the Noratlas, which had parked next to the hangar they had sought refuge in. The MPLA group were told that the Noratlas had come to collect luggage of Portuguese military personnel returning to the Metropolis. When the FNLA fighters were safely concealed in the luggage the FAP crew came back to the bar and told Moutinho it was time to leave the base. Still concealed in the Noratlas the FNLA group were taken to a part of Angola which they still controlled. Captain Moutinho said he had seen the film *Raid on Entebbe* a few weeks previously which gave him some inspiration for the FNLA rescue! Angola's three guerrilla armies lost around 3,200 fighters in the war which took the lives of around 50 FAP pilots and aircrew and about 1,500 Portuguese troops.

Extra images for Angola section.

*mini-brake pedals on Portuguese Auster. C Barrett at Museu
do Ar*

*Over BA6, near Lisbon, one of 5 FAP Broussards sent to Angola
in 61. FAP*

Puma over Angola. FAP

Puma in northern Angola. F Cruz.

Troops transfer to Unimog trucks from Pumas. F Cruz.

Nearly all Esq 94 Pumas. F Cruz

First FAP Al 2 in Angola in 1961. FAP

Pilots with Pumas that collided at Toto. F Cruz.

Al 3 recovers Do-27 in Angola. FAP

Esq 94 Al3s near Luanda. FAP

FAV Austers in Ambriz, Angola. R Duarte

Capt Moutinho with Do-27 in Angola. F Moutinho

The last Thunderjet pilot Victor Silva at BA9 in 73. V Silva

Thunderjet gets JATO boost at BA9. F Moutinho

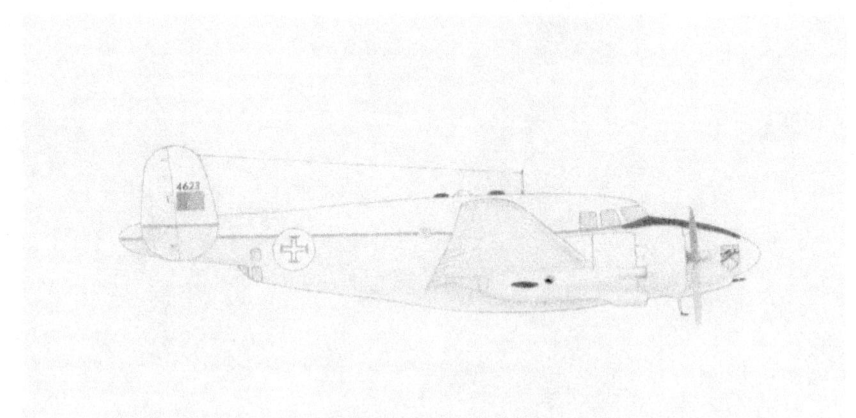

Esq 91 Harpoon. I Strange

Mucaba Chapel seige survivors. Unknown credit.

Slightly angled Harpoon. I Strange

Esq 91 Harpoon in Angola. FAP

Kids and pals of FAV pilot João Duarte by his Auster. R Duarte

FAV pilots and a PIper Cub. R Duarte

Patch of first FAV sq with motto "loyalty and courage"

Joåo Duarte's Tiger Moth. R Duarte

*New strip in northern Angola opened by J Duarte. R
Duarte*

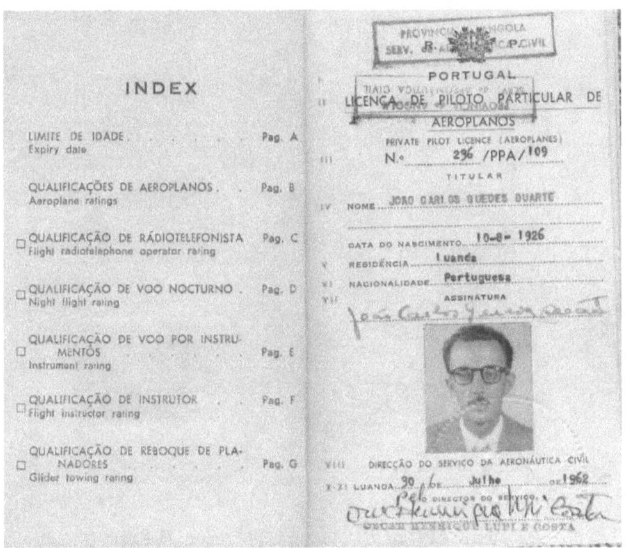

J Duarte's pilot license. R Duarte

Noratlas over Luanda. FAP

Al 2 and kids of Angolan FAV pilot. R Duarte

Heli-canão ready for mission at BA9. F Cruz

Gunner's view of another Al3 dropping troop. F Cruz

2 Esq 94 AL3 in north. F Cruz

B-26 with olive green anti-radiation paint at BA9

B-26 on mission in northern Angola. B Neves

*MPLA chief Agostinho Neto, left, in Morocco training camp.
MSF.*

UNITA leader Jonas Savimbi in 1970. I Lippman.

B-26 at BA9 in 72. FAP

Civilians leave Huambo Airport in 75. I Lippman

Esq 94 Puma nearly hits trees probably due to pilot fatigue. FAP

"office" of Puma over Angola. M Silva

MPLA founder Mario Pinto de Andrade posing with Kalash-nikov. MSF

Esq 94 Pumas in 71. F Cruz

MOD. 417-D J. A.

REGIÃO MILITAR DE ANGOLA

(A) BATALHÃO DE CAÇADORES Nº442

(B) Secretaria

S.F.M.3796

Nota nº175-Pºu6

Ao Sr.

PRESIDENTE DO AERO CLUB DE AMBRIZ

AMBRIZ

S/ REFERÊNCIA   S/ COMUNICAÇÃO DE   N/ REFERÊNCIA Nota nº175-Pºu6   (C)

ASSUNTO :

É com a maior satisfação que me dirijo a V.Exª para manifestar o nosso profundo reconhecimento ao Aero Club de Ambriz, pela assiduidade que o vosso avião vem a muxaluando prestando um inestimável serviço de transporte de correio, que tanto eleva o moral das tropas.

Ainda gostosamente desejo informar V.Exª a grande amabilidade, com que o respectivo piloto Sr. Duarte, se prontifica a satisfazer todos os pedidos que lhe são dirigidos inclusive efde pequenos reconhecimentos aéreos sobre as nossas tropas para as localizar no campo, e as preciosas informações sobre algumas concentrações de terroristas que referênci nas suas viagens.

Aproveitando a oportunidade endereço a V.Exª os protest da mais elevada consideração.

A BEM DA NAÇÃO

O COMANDANTE

JOAQUIM GOUVEIA
TEN.COR.

Thank-you letter from local Army chief to Joao Duarte. R Duarte

FAV pilots at airstrip dedicated to soldier killed in UPA raids. R Duarte

Dornier doing risky Congo River touch-and-go. FAP

UNITA fighter in 70. I Lippman

An Al 3 supplied by South Africa in southern Angola. FAP

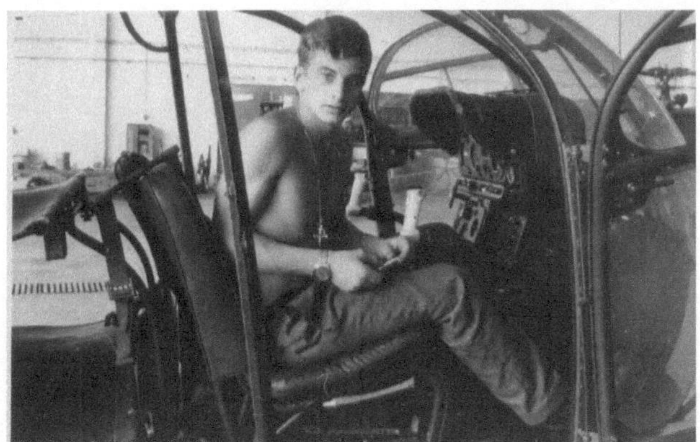

Al 3 in main hangar at BA 9. F Cruz

Dornier and T-6 at Gago Coutinho base in Angola with 80kg napalm bombs. FAP

"The guerrilla walks free on the ground while the little Portuguese flies high commanding the clouds." PAIGC marching song.

Guinea-Bissau, to the south of Senegal and west of Republic of Guinea – both former French colonies – is about a fifth bigger than Belgium and had a population of around 600,000 in 1961. It was described as a grim, torrid stretch of swamp and jungle by Al Venter, the South African writer who was one of the few foreign journalists authorised to cover Portugal's African wars. Guinea has no natural wealth, unlike Angola and Mozambique, and most of its population survived on growing ground nuts. It is a complex territory to project force into, and therefore challenging to safeguard from internal and external threats from porous frontiers on all sides

The first armed attacks against Portugal's overseas territory of Guinea-Bissau occurred in July 1961 when the Movimento de Libertação da Guiné (MLG) launched raids from the north in neighbouring Senegal. Portuguese troops were sent to dissuade more MLG raids. As part of the military reaction to the MLG, eight FAP F-86F Sabres, and two in reserve, were sent on 9 August from the Montijo base near Lisbon to AB2 in Bissalanca, the main civil and military airfield outside the Guinean capital, Bissau, in an operation dubbed Atlas with a 3,704 km journey for the US-supplied jets under the MDP. The F-86Fs were fitted with 200 gallon tanks on each internal hard point and another two 120 gallon tanks on the external ones to give maximum range for the longest leg of 1,481 km from Grand Canaria to Sal (AT1) in the Cape Verde archipelago, one of Portugal's African territories. The AT1 base in Cape Verde was a strategic one both for Portugal's African empire and also international obligations for SAR operations off West Africa by the FAP and Portuguese Navy.

The ten FAP pilots slept overnight in the Canaries before departing for Sal, where they were delayed for several days because of bad weather. It was the first rainfall in seven years in drought-stricken Cape Verde. The Sabres, all part of *Destacamento* 5, or Detachment

5, finally arrived in Guinea on 15 July to a badly maintained 6,000 ft runway and a small FAP hangar adjacent to the modest civil terminal.

Before the arrival of the F-86Fs, the FAP had two Dakotas, two Austers and four T-6Gs but these aircraft were virtually incapable of being operated. The flight of F-86Fs at AB 2 was under the command of Flight Captain Almeida Santos and the FAP had decided to rotate its pilots in Guinea every three months to give vital experience of Africa, which at this stage virtually none of its 300-odd pilots had any experience of. Armed with six .50-calibre machine guns, four 2.75-inch rockets and two bombs of up to 454 kg, the first Sabre familiarisation sorties from AB2 were on 19 August when Flight Lieutenant Teixeira Lobo in serial 5361 suffered a bird strike and the jet would be out of action for several weeks so another F-86F was dispatched from Portugal.

FAP Sabre at Bissalanca with rockets and bombs. FAP

In the early part of the Sabres deployment to Guinea, they mainly undertook reconnaissance and armed reconnaissance missions and faced some navigational problems as they were using obsolete maps so could have easily flown into Senegal's airspace on the missions against the MLG. The radio aids to navigation in Guinea were still crude, with a sole radio beacon at AB2 and no possibility of instrument approaches. But new VHF and UHF transceivers were installed at the main FAP airbase, which also had to handle some civil traffic from neighbouring West African states and sometimes further afield like Lisbon. But it was not uncommon for the F-86F pilots to abort an approach to AB2 when an unidentified aircraft came into the pattern. Runway safety at the base was still in the process of being improved and a local resident wandered onto the runway and a few days later cattle appeared on the downwind apron. Both incidents resulted in aborted landings by the newly arrived jets.

The flight of Sabres in Guinea had a few other operating problems, like further bird strikes and a lack of oxygen to supply the aircraft systems, but by October 1961 – and the close of the rainy season – readiness for the F-84Fs stood at 100% for all aircraft. In the same month, the maiden group of pilots in Destacamento 5, about to return to Portugal on leave, gave a six-ship display over Bissau and Flight Lieutenant Lobo in serial 5322 managed to break the sound barrier in a shallow dive! However, the initial Sabre operations during 1961 in Guinea had been hamstrung by the pilots' lack of ability to communicate by radio with ground troops, so the jets could only undertake pre-planned attacks on insurgent sites. But the FAP's handful of T-6s carried the PRC-10, a UHF FM transceiver, which was also the main radio used by the Portuguese Army, so the T-6G was used both in CAS of Navy and Army patrols.

The first FAP aircraft lost in Guinea was a T-6G on 29 May 1962, when Flight Lieutenant José Neves and Flight Sergeant Manuel de Matos lost their lives after crashing into the Corubal River while inspecting canoes of suspected MLG fighters. Most of the F-86F flights from AB2 during 1962 were sovereignty flights in northern Guinea to deter guerrilla activity, and the first aircraft lost

T-6 downed by PAIGC. A Cabral

was on 17 August when Flight Captain Gomes do Amaral and his wingman Fight Lieutenant Amílcar Barbosa ran into torrential rain on the return to BA 2, Bissalanca. Do Amaral managed to land his Sabre but the other jet made a number of unsuccessful attempts before crashing into a hill beyond the main runway with the jet ending up on its side. The pilot, however, escaped with minor injuries, but his F-86F was written off.

In 1963, one FAP F-86 was shot down by Partido Africano da Independência da Guiné e Cabo Verde (PAIGC) ground fire but the pilot ejected and was recovered. The PAIGC had made its first deadly attacks on Portuguese troops the same year in the west of Guinea in an uprising that soon put the PAIGC ahead in the hearts and minds game, faced with a divided and inflexible Portuguese armed forces command still seeking a purely military solution to the uprising. In late 1964, the FAP F-86Fs flew their final missions in Guinea because Portugal had come under American pressure to repatriate the 16 jets because use in the African counter-insurgency war contravened the agreement under which they were supplied by the US: to be used solely for the defence of NATO's southwestern Western flank and not used in Portuguese Africa.

"Tell no lies and claim to easy victories" A. Cabral

Additionally, Portugal's new and more potent guerrilla adversary in Guinea, the PAIGC, had complained to Washington that the US-supplied jets were being used to attack its fighters in Guinea. The PAIGC was formed in 1956 by Amilcar Cabral and promoted a dockworkers' strike in 1959 which was brutally broken by Portuguese troops with 50 workers killed. Cabral, an agronomist by profession who of the Guinean independence organisation, was primarily a nationalist rather than a follower of the Marxist-Leninist ideas of most other contemporary guerrilla leaders. He went to university in Lisbon and was among only 14 Africans in Guinea to have a degree. The former Soviet Union was the main supplier of arms to the PAIGC but its fighters also trained in China, Algeria and Czechoslovakia and had some Cuban advisors.

Cabral travelled extensively around Guinea gathering support for the independence struggle, which was unlike most other contemporary African insurgencies launched from neighbouring states or mountainous regions. During the guerrilla campaign, Cabral often said the PAIGC needed to convert Guineans themselves into the mountains needed in the fight against Lisbon's colonial rule.

A costly day for the PAIGC and its foreign supporters

In 1969, on 6 January at 08:45, BA 12 got a request for the QRA G 91s to go to Gadamel Porto, where a large group of PAIGC, including vehicles, were attacking the base. The PAIGC had always launched raids on bases towards dusk and used the darkness to evade Portuguese troops and FAP aircraft. Two Esquadra 121 Fiats with the usual QRA cocktail of 8 70mm SNEB rockets, four .5 calibre machine guns and extra fuel tanks were dispatched southwards at 09:00 to Gadamel Porto, and it was assumed the PAIGC force would take cover or disperse in the presence of the two attack jets.

Sole PAIGC Zis-2 deployment. C Cabral

It had been reported that the guerrillas were using two unidentified anti-tank guns, on wheels and with long barrels, to shell the Gademel Porto base. A local Portuguese army patrol had engaged the PAIGC group with an 81mm mortar as well as the artillery in the Gadamel Porto base, and the FAP G 91 pair were notified of the presumed coordinates of the PAIGC's new weapon, at Bricama about 2k SW of Gadamel Porto. The Fiats flew to Bricama but as they overflew the abandoned Sangonha base they were astonished to see hundreds of PAIGC troops in the former base, which had an airstrip, and were even more concerned that a ZPU-4 had opened fire on them.

The G-91s flew in circles for a few minutes outside range of the ZPU-4 and its 2,400 rounds per minute, and the lead pilot decided not to attack because heavier weapons than rockets were required and a swift decision at BA 12 would be needed on which bomb configuration would be necessary to take out the ZPU-4 and the two new anti-tank guns in the former Sangonha base, which had been demolished with explosives a few months earlier to stymie is PAIGC use.

The anti-tank guns being used by the PAIGC were WW2 vintage Russian Zis-2 57mm on wheels, it would later transpire. They were a brand-new weapon in the PAIGC arsenal but would never be used again in Guinea against Portuguese forces. The QRA Fiats were back at BA 12 about 45 minutes after their departure to respond to the unprecedented daylight PAIGC raid, which the Portuguese military command in Guinea assumed would be withdrawn into cover of trees or retreat to neighbouring Republic of Guinea before it could be attacked with FAP bombs.

An Alouette 3 helicopter attack with 30 Paras was the first option considered but it would take too long and jeopardise the lives of the special forces personnel , as well as risk precious helicopters and FAP pilots and aircrew. Some Fiats were involved in other operations that day so the only Esquadra 121 G 91s available was the QRA pair that had just returned to BA 12 and another two at the base. Because the full 600 kg bomb load could not be used without removing the Fiat's fuel tanks, which would waste precious minutes, it was decided to arm each jet with two 200 kg bombs and two 50 kg ones.

The four Esquadra 121 Fiats left BA 12 around 11:00, about three hours after the initial PAIGC shelling of the Gadamel Porto base and their oc-cupation of Sangonha, so it was highly likely that the guerrillas and the ZPU-4 and two anti-tank guns had left the scene in fear of being spotted by the FAP again. Flight Colonel Diogo Neto led the four G 91s up to 8,000 at 400 knots, the habitual

Fiat with bombs at BA 12. J Nico

altitude and speed for bombing runs to begin. The Fiats bombed the PAIGC position in quick succession from about 200 ft and none met any AAA resistance. The Esquadra 121 jets were soon back in Bissalanca at BA 12 and it would be another three days before an army patrol would make a careful inspection, supported by a Dornier DO-27, of the abandoned base at Sangonha.

In the three days following the seemingly suicidal PAIGC attack on Sangonha, local Portuguese Army units and the Gadamel Porto base had kept a keen watch for any more guerrilla activity or bombardments, but none occurred. To learn the fate of the large PAIGC group and its AAA and other weapons that had been seen on January 6, it was decided to send a group of 100 troops and local trackers to the area and at 08:30 a Dornier

Do-27 was dispatched from BA 12 to survey the area and also provide top cover to two T6Gs, armed with rockets and machine guns, in case of any guerrilla attacks on the reconnaissance party. A strong odour of decomposing human flesh and the presence of vultures was the first indication the Portuguese troops and trackers had reached the site of the bombing by the four Esquadra 121 G 91s a few days earlier.

Sixteen makeshift graves were found as well as many body parts that were both white and black. The two Zis-2 anti-tank cannons were also discovered totally destroyed in the abandoned base as well as part of the potent ZPU-4 that had fired briefly on the two Esquadra 121 Fiats. Local officials later confirmed that around 400 people had been in a road convoy, including an ambulance, to Sanhonha on January 6. At the time, Portugal's intelligence services believed the PAIGC were making a propaganda film with Swedish support that day. Swedish filmmakers, photographers and Cuban PAIGC supporters and advisors would have been among the party and would also account for some of the body parts found at the scene.

The suicidal attack was made during daylight because at the time it wasn't possible to film at night without heavy and cumbersome lighting equipment. The PAIGC opted to use the large vintage Russian gun, with a long barrel, instead of the less photogenic 88m mortars or RPGs, their weapons of choice, because it would have appeared more dramatic in the final footage of the already derelict Portuguese base being taken by the guerillas.

In 1969 Sweden had become the first Western state to support independence movements in Portugal's African territories and became the largest contributor of non-lethal assistance to the PAIGC. While the Soviet Union supplied most of the PAIGC's arms, Sweden donated the equivalent of USD 4 million between 1969 and 1975 for social services, healthcare, and education to the independence movement on the basis it controlled most of the state's territory.

Robust West German relations and an Italian-made jet to the rescue

The PAIGC had opened its first front in Guinea in 1962 in the south and in 1963, with backing from Senegal, began attacking Portuguese troops in the north and a year later it started using the Republic of Guinea to launch raids from the east. The PAIGC attacks usually involved its fighters starting to march at dawn into Guinea from their neighbouring sanctuaries and approaching the Portuguese bases and positions towards dusk to launch their attacks under the cover of darkness.

The principal PAIGC weapons were the Soviet-supplied 82mm mortar with a maximum range of 3,000 metres, which could be disassembled into several parts and had a fire rate of 15 to 25 rounds a minute. Each projectile weighed 3 kg and the mortar ammunition was carried in crate of ten rounds weighing about 30 kg. About six insurgents were required to carry the weapon and its ammunition before the average attack.

In 1971 the Soviet Union started supplying the PAIGC with the 122m "Grad" rockets. The new weapon had its own units with eight personnel per launcher. The two Grads operated in a single unit of two launchers and 16 PAIGC fighters. The normal PAIGC order of battle was for between 38 and 44 men with 4 rocket-propelled grenades (RPG) five light-machines guns (LMG). When the 82mm mortar was being used, there would be between 50 and 70 guerrillas in the group.

The PAIGC would develop a diverse and potent artillery during its long war with Portugal and the jewel in the crown in this department was the Obusier 155m howitzer with a 18,000 metre effective range, supplied by Sweden. The departure of the F-86s left the T-6G as the sole FAP attack aircraft in Guinea for 20 months until the advent of a Sabre replacement. Faced with reduced FAP bombing capacities in Guinea while the Sabres were being replaced, one of three Douglas C-47S at BA 12 were fitted with bomb racks to carry 50 kg and 200 kg bombs and a smaller bombs and grenades tube in the cabin floor to drop small bombs and grenades on night missions.

The Dakotas would soon see action alongside the new aircraft when they eventually arrived. The other FAP aircraft at BA 12 were 20 Dornier DO-27 utility aircraft and nine Alouette 3 helicopters, all part of Grupo Operacional 1201 (GO 1201) at BA 12. Some of the DO-27s, whose short takeoff and landing (STOL) capacity was ideal for Guinea's dozens of short strips, were fitted with 37mm anti-personnel rocket pods, and the German planes were also used for reconnaissance, liaison, resupply and forward air control. The DO-27 had a minimum flying speed of 28 MPH and 460 feet takeoff run, and after the T6 had the second-highest rate of FAP aircrew deaths in combat and accidents.

The Alouette 3s of Esquadra 122, based at BA 12, were used for medevac, troop insertion, resupply and reconnaissance. Its gunship version was equipped with a Matra MG1-51 cannon mounted in the rear left-side door, known in Guinea as *Lobo Mau* in Portuguese: Big Bad Wolf. Portugal's military was the first to be supplied by France with the Alouette 3 and had developed the fearsome gunship in Angola after experimenting with various machine gun configurations. In its own counterinsurgency wars, Rhodesia followed the Portuguese example by installing MG-151s in its Alouette 3s, known as the K-Car.

The peak FAP deployment of Alouettes in Guinea was 21 machines in 1970. PAIGC soldiers feared the FAP helicopters so much, particularly the gunship version, that Amilcar Cabral drew up a tactics primer on how to engage rotary-wing aircraft. In the absence of the Sabre's potent bombing and strafing threat for nearly two years, the PAIGC managed to bolster its the fighting capacities in the south and north of Guinea and increase their support from the population as well as build an effective network of anti-aircraft artillery (AAA).

However, after months of fruitless searching by Portugal among NATO partners for an F-86F replacement. West Germany agreed to sell 40 G-91 R/4 attack jets that would not be affected by a UN arms embargo on Portugal's African wars. From the early 1960s. West Germany and Portugal had developed defence cooperation whereby Bonn would support Portugal's defence industry and also supply surplus aircraft like the Nord Aviation Noratalas transporter and Dornier DO-27s. The FAP received 300 aircraft from West Germany throughout the 1960s and Bonn continued to supply munitions and materiel to Portugal's military for use in its African wars, which many countries refused to supply arms to.

The Luftwaffe Fiats, manufactured under license in Germany, had been mothballed and were refurbished while the FAP trained pilots on the new jets. The first nine Fiats had arrived by November 1966 in separate sea shipments and were assigned to a newly created squadron, Esquadra 121 (Esq 121) Tigres, or Tigers. The compact Fiat jets, with Bristol Siddeley Orpheus turbojets that also powered the Foland Gnat, had been designed to use roads as runways and could operate from poorly maintained strips.

The G 91 R/4 used by the FAP was identical to the R/1 version used by the Italian Air Force with an additional two underwing hard-points and the same avionics as the Luftwaffe's R/3 version. The Portuguese Fiats had a maximum bomb load of 680 kg, comprising two 340 kg bombs on the wing root stations. They could also carry eight SNEB 70mm rockets on the outboard stations or four 50 kg bombs in place of the rockets.

Fiat with bombs leaving BA12. J Nico

The most common weapons configuration was four outboard 50 kg bombs with two 200 kg ones on the inner stations. Two 320 litre external fuel tanks could be carried on the root station and the G.91 was also armed with four 0.5-calibre machine guns with 300 rounds apiece. As BA 12 was roughly in the centre of Guinea and the G 91 had a 50-minute endurance without extra fuel tanks, it could carry a full 680 kg bomb load on ground attack missions. But as rockets were the most useful close support weapon because they didn't compromise the Fiat's manoeuvrability, they were usually the weapon of choice, along with the two external tanks, in these operations. A pair of Quick Reaction Alert (QRA) G 91s at BA 12 normally used the rocket and extra fuel configuration. The 70mm rockets could be fired in pairs or in salvo and were general purpose rather than the anti-personnel ones carried by the T-6G and Do-27, so more versatile.

The Esquadra 121 Fiats used general purpose, demolition and fragmentation bombs, depending on the targets, and two 300 litre napalm canisters were carried on the root stations. Napalm was mainly used against PAIGC AAA sites, bases and other structures and was usually confined to the dry season in Guinea, running from November to May. Declassified FAP documents on napalm use in Guinea from late 1968 to Feb 1973 show that 40 300-litre bombs per month were used on average and 42 80-litre ones. The Fiats were also an ideal reconnaissance platform with vertical and oblique cameras that were used to locate PAIGC anti-aircraft batteries and bases in neighbouring states and infiltration routes.

The initial objective of the new G 91 squadron was to destroy the PAIGC AAA emplacements built up in the south of Guinea as well as interdict enemy movement on roads, trails and rivers, especially ones coming from Republic of Guinea. On their first missions over southern Guinea, the Esquadra 121 Fiats attracted intense fire from ZPU-1 12.7mm single and ZPU 4 14.5mm single and multi-barrelled heavy machine guns introduced by the PAIGC fighters in the summer of 1966, assisted by highly experienced Cuban advisors.

Most of the G 91 missions in the remaining months of the year were armed reconnaissance, although in operation *Estoque*, the jets worked with T6Gs and the C-47 Dakota bomber to attack anti-aircraft positions. Two Fiats received hits from the ZPU-4 heavy machine guns on these missions and in early 1967 six G 91 joined 11 T6 and seven Alouette 3 carrying paratroopers in an operation to destroy PAIGC guns around the River Geba.

The quad-barrel ZPU-4 used a four-wheel carriage and was quickly lowered into its firing jacks in around 15 seconds to fire around 2,400 rounds per minute. It was fondly referred to as quatro bocas by its mainly Cuban operators – although a few PAIGC troops also operated them – and had a range up to 15,000 ft, which was only effective up to 4,600 ft. The twin-barrel ZPU-2 used by the PAIGC as mobile AAA had

PAIGC with ZPU-4. A Cabral

two wheels that were removed in the firing position and the single-barrel ZPU-1 had a two-wheel carriage that was disassembled into several 80 kg pieces when crossing rough ground, or rivers in PAIGC canoes.

By February 1967, Esquadra 121 lost its first Fiat after Flight Major Santos Morreira's aircraft, 5407, was damaged from the blast of its own bombs. Guided by his wingman, Morreira tried to return to BA 12 but was forced to eject before reaching Bissalanca. A shortage of bombs until 1968 meant the G 91 attacks on PAIGC gunners were often made with low-level single bomb passes on the enemy's foxholes usually less than two metres in diameter. This single pass bombing method proved difficult and dangerous for the Fiat pilots but when sufficient amounts of 200 kg and 50 kg bombs arrived in early 1968, the tactic changed to a 600 kg load drop in one high-speed pass.

A wave of five Fiats dropping the maximum load in succession was often sufficient to destroy the AAA and cause the guerrillas to flee. In 1968, Portuguese cavalry general António de Spínola, took over as Guinea's governor and military commander and launched a belated drive to develop the impoverished colony and take the fight to the PAIGC. Spinola also decided the enemy AA sites in southern Guinea were still a threat.

In a joint forces operation in April 1969 to take out six ZPU-1 and one ZPU-4, two G 91s and a Do-27 were damaged but managed to return to BA 12. As a consequence, Esquadra 121 was reinforced to have 12 Fiats. In July 1968, Esquadra 121 lost its second Fiat when Flight Lieutenant Costa Gomes in G 91 5411 was hit by ZPU-1 fire near an Army garrison. Lieutenant Colonel Gomes ejected and proceeded to the base, whose sentry refused to believe he was a pilot as he looked too old.

PAIGC gets Soviet game changer

The G 91s continued to monitor and regularly attack the PAIGC heavy machine guns for three more years until 1970 when Soviet-supplied 37mm anti-aircraft cannons were introduced by the enemy to claw back a little advantage over the FAP. But until 1973, when a potent game-changing weapon unexpectedly came into the PAIGC inventory, the FAP maintained air supremacy in Guinea to support Portuguese ground troops, evacuate wounded soldiers, resupply bases and closely monitor PAIGC troop movements and anti-aircraft batteries using the G 91 reconnaissance cameras.

After two FAP T6s were buzzed by MIG 17Fs of the Republic of Guinea Air Force near Guinea's southern border region in April 1968, and amid rumours the PAIGC was creating its own air force, with pilots trained in the Soviet Union, the Chief of Staff of the Air Force (CEMFA) instructed BA 12 to urgently review its radar and AA defences. The FAP had lost its air-to-air defence capacity when the Sabres were recalled to Portugal and it was decided the G 91 could not be used as a fighter after a test installation of AIM-9B Sidewinder air-to-air missiles and a K-14 computing gyro gunsight proved unsuccessful.

Portugal ordered Crotale missiles from France in 1974 and was also supplied with American FIM-43A Redeye missiles via Israel. But the French air defence system only arrived in the final months of the war in Guinea. The Russian-made SAM-7 was first used in combat in 1969 by the Egyptian troops against Israeli aircraft. In early 1972, the missile made its debut in the Vietnam War after North Vietnamese regular soldiers used the highly portable shoulder-launched system against US aircraft.

By June, 45 US aircraft were lost to the SAM-7, and the missile was recognised as a serious threat to all aircraft, especially helicopters and slow flying aircraft. After reading reports of the SAM-7 use in Vietnam, PAICG leader Amilcar Cabral visited Moscow in June 1973 to request delivery of the weapon to challenge Portugal's air superiority in Guinea, which he saw as the sole military reason Lisbon was clinging to the colony. Cabral was assassinated in January 1973 by a PAIGC rival who was in the pay of Portugal's feared PIDE political police, and at his funeral, a Russian Soviet official informed the new PAIGC leadership that the missile request had been granted and a group of fighters should be sent to Russia for training.

The first SAM-7 arrived in Conakry in the Republic of Guinea in March and would be used within a week. On 20 March, the PAIGC made its first SAM-7 firing at a G 91 flown by Flight Lieutenant Colonel José Brito in northern Guinea. The missile missed but neither the pilot nor his wingman Flight Lieutenant Miguel Pessoa realised they were dealing with a new enemy weapon. Two days later, the PAIGC fired another SAM-7 at a Dornier Do-27 that also missed. The Dornier pilot, however, called for a strike on the suspected launch site and two G 91s responded but were both targeted by missiles as well as a third Fiat sent to the location.

Lt Pessoa and special forces. D Rodriques.

The PAIGC SAM-7 teams would not shoot down a FAP aircraft until March 25 when Flight Lieutenant Pessoa's Fiat 5413 took the full impact of a missile while flying at 1,000 feet to repel a PAIGC attack on the Guiledge garrison in northern Guinea. The PAIGC had shelled the Portuguese Army base in expectation the FAP would dispatch a Fiat and the guerrillas were anxious to bring down a Portuguese plane after days of misses. Pessoa lost engine power and flight controls and with the G 91 sinking, quick ejected at low level and suffered a leg fracture after landing on a tree. Pessoa spent 20 hours hiding in thick forest avoiding capture, but the PAIGC military commander, João Bernardo Vieira, said his men were celebrating their first SAM-7 kill so much they hadn't noticed Pessoa's low-level ejection. The downed FAP pilot fired a flare in the evening that was seen by a searching Fiat flown by Lieutenant Colonel Brito and special forces were sent the next day to bring Pessoa back to BA 12 by Alouette 3s.

Despite Esquadra 121 commander Flight Lieutenant Colonel Brito's close encounter with the new extremely dangerous weapon a few days ago, he continued to believe the PAIGC were using rocket-propelled grenades to attack the FAP aircraft. He had also been informed by Portugal's intelligence services that the PAIGC would be supplied with the missiles. Tragically, Brito was the SAM-7's first victim on 28 March when his G 91 5419 was hit on a bombing raid at Madina do Boe. April 6 was the costliest day of the war in Guinea for the FAP with two Do-27s and a T6 hit by SAM-7s, killing three pilots and four servicemen. A third Do-7 was damaged by the shockwave of a missile but managed to limp back to BA 12.

One of the aircrew on the surviving Do-7 was Giselda Antunes, one of the FAP's elite unit of all-female para-nurses. The 48 nurses were also qualified to parachute and use weapons if necessary. Antunes had been aboard the Alouette 3 on Lieutenant Miguel Pessoa's dramatic recovery from the jungle and they married after the war in Lisbon. Miguel and Giselda Pessoa are believed to be the only couple in the world to have survived separate SAM attacks and they organise regular reunions and dinners for ex-combatants from Guinea.

The FAP suspended all operations in Guinea for at least two days after losing three aircraft on April 6 but helicopters and piston-engined T6 and Do-27 continued to fly but with fewer sorties while the FAP devised new operational procedures to deal with the SAM-7 threat. The consequent lack of medevac and close-support in this period lowered moral of Portuguese troops and resulted in the PAIGC taking control of more parts of Guinea.

Brito's Fiat with PAIGC guards. A Cabral

The appearance of the SAM-7 in the skies of Guinea obliged the FAP to gather information about the Soviet missiles' capabilities and limitations, and Portugal's intelligence service, the DGS, obtains information from Germany's foreign intelligence agency, the BND, that the SA-7 couldn't engage targets under 160 to 190 ft and above 5,000 ft. It soon emerged that the weapon could lock onto targets at up to 8,000 ft, however. Fixed-wing aircraft and helicopters could avoid the missile by evasive manoeuvres and staying below 190 ft or above 8,000 ft.

Armed with the new information on the SAM-7's limitations, Esquadra 121 changed the Fiat's bomb run procedure to a descent from 10,000 ft with bomb release at 6,000 ft and the lowest point of the trajectory at 2,500 ft. Working in pairs, the second G 91 stays above the missile range to scout the ground and the airspace around the other jet and warning by radio of missile firings. The SAM7 produced a large cloud of white smoke from its ignition and a smoke trail from its solid fuel engine which gave away its trajectory. If an FAP pilot saw the missile approaching, he could get away from its infrared sensor's relatively narrow range by a sudden change in altitude and heading.

But the new higher bombing altitude meant targets were often missed by a wide margin. The FAP lost another G 91 in September when Flight Captain Carlos Wanzeller's jet, 5416, supporting a helicopter insertion using 750 pound (340kg) bombs, rolls suddenly left to become inverted, subjecting the pilot to excessive acceleration and denying him control of the aircraft. After a momentarily loss of consciousness, Wanzeller ejects, to be later recovered by a helicopter involved in the operation. The following investigation of the accident finds no reason for the loss of control, with the pilot exonerated of any fault.

Esquadra 121 lost another G 91 in October when Flight Captain Alberto Cruz in 5409 lost control of his aircraft at the end of a bombing run. The pilot ejected at around 400 knots, which is close to the Martin Baker drogue chute rupture limit 470 knots. Cruz lost his helmet in the violent ejection and reached the ground quickly. The other Fiat pilot alerts BA 12 in Bissalanca what has happened and two Alouette 3 gunships, with another two Fiats as top cover, rescued Captain Cruz. It later emerged that a machine gun ammunition panel on the side of the aircraft had opened in flight, making the G 91 highly unstable.

A PAIGC SAM-7 operator who surrendered to the Portuguese in October 1973 said the lack of success against the G 91 was because of difficulties in acquiring the target in a dive and also the tendency of pilots to exit a bombing or strafing run in a very tight turn, surpassing the manoeuvring capacity of the missile. Another excellent evasive manoeuvre practiced by the FAP Fiat pilots was to strafe in a dive and abandon the pass in a corkscrew manoeuvre until just above treetop level. This meant the aircraft's tailpipe, the source of infrared emissions, was more concealed than on attack runs finishing in a climb. But bombing from 6,000 ft resulted in PAIGC targets being missed by a long chalk and the bombs sometimes falling harmlessly into rivers or even the sea.

One FAP mission obliged to fly under 100 ft with the new orders on altitudes to avoid SA-7 attacks was a medevac in November 1973 when para-nurse Giselda Antunes and her colleague Natalia Santos were dispatched from BA 12 in Bisssalanca to Catio in a Do-27. To avoid PAIGC-controlled zones, the pilot Flight Sergeant Ivo Mota flew along the coast but the Dornier's engine suddenly lost all power and Mota was forced to bring the plane down in thick mud because it was low tide. The Dornier's propeller had struck a bird the previous day but the machine was inspected and cleared to fly.

None of the crew were injured in Mota's skilful landing but the trio were in an enemy stronghold and they could see African faces looking at them from the shore about 700 metres away so they moved to find deeper water to hide themselves. But Mota decided to return to the Dornier to retrieve a pistol kept under its rear seat for personal protection of FAP aircrew. The pilot needed assistance from Giselda Antunes to return to the aircraft and when they left it, they had difficulty finding Natalia Santos, the other para-nurse.

Medevac Do-27 recovery. FAP

Meanwhile at BA12 it had been noticed that there were no reports from the Dornier medevac mission for some time so a Fiat G-91 was dispatched to fly along its route. The Dornier was spotted by the Fiat jet and the Portuguese Navy sent a patrol to locate the three FAP personnel.

On 31 January 1974, Flight Lieutenant Castro Gil's G 91 was hit by a SAM-7 as it climbed away from guerrillas attacking a northern Army base near the frontier with Senegal. Gil ejected and landed near enemy lines and kept moving through the night to evade PAIGC troops on his trail. Portuguese special forces started searching for Gil the next morning and found his parachute and ejection seat but no signs of the pilot. A Do-27 sent to find Gil failed to see his flare and he eventually persuaded some friendly villagers to take him on the rear seat of a bicycle to an Army base, from where he was flown by C-47 to AB 12 in the evening. A party in honour of Gil left him confined to the base's military hospital for being drunk and a nurse coming on duty, not knowing about the pilot's ordeal, decided to confine him to the psychiatric ward!

The PAIGC had a monopoly on guerrilla-operated SAM-7s for a few weeks because in May 1973 the Palestinian Liberation Organisation (PLO) received the missile which they used to bring down an Israeli F-4 fighter in the October 1973 war. The weapon also reportedly entered the arms caches of the Provisional Irish Republican Army (PIRA) supplied by Libya. As part of its strategy to protect the G 91s from the SAM-7 threat, the FAP acquired dark green low-reflection paint for the planes from France. The Fiat's Christ Cross roundels were also reduced in size for the same reason. TRACOR TBC-72 flare dispensers were also bought for the Fiats with a plan to fit four per plane near the trailing edge of the internal weapons pylons. The US system allowed use of thermal flares and chaff but was not fitted to the G 91s because of the 25 April 1974 Revolution in Portugal, which hastened the end of the wars in Guinea, Angola and Mozambique.

The Lisbon coup was led by left-wing war-weary junior Army officers and swiftly restored full democracy to Portugal. A ceasefire with the PAIGC was signed in May 1974. The guerrillas lost up to 2,000 men in the conflict and became Guinea's ruling party on independence, with Luis Cabral, half-brother of Amilcar Cabral, becoming president. The 11-year war in Guinea claimed the lives of 61 FAP personnel, including pilots, observers, para-nurses and paratroopers. Some 505 FAP servicemen and women were killed in the three African theatres from a total 9,274 Portuguese military deaths.

BA12 from above. Civil terminal beyond military. J Nico

Extra images for Guinea section

PAIGC SA-7 operator. I Strange

66mm SNEB pod on experimental Alouette in 73 in Guinea. D Silva.

Same test chopper with T-6 machine guns and 37mm pods and G-91 gunsight. D Silva

T-6 at BA12 having machine guns armed. J Nico

Nice snap of T-6 from Alouette 3. J Nico

PAIGC RPG. A Cabral

Young Guinean woman with Swedish medic. A Cabral

Impressive Fiat flight-line at BA12. J Nico

First Fiat in Guinea serial 5401 in 68. FAP

Nice study of PAIGC canoe patrol. A Cabral.

AK-47 PAIGC with porters. A Cabral

60mm Chinese mortar. A Cabral

750lb and other bombs at BA 12. FAP

T-6 with bombs and rockets over Guinea. J Nico

PAIGC 57mm anti-tank gun. A Cabral

Fighters with Degtyararev machine gun. A Cabral

French COIN expert G Chaliand interviewing Osvaldo Vieira of PAIGC. A Cabral

Al 3 medevac Nova Lamego covered by gunship. FAP

Cabral after recent China trip. A Cabral

100kg bombs on Fiat at BA12. J Nico

PPSh-41-toting PAIGC greets local. A Cabral

Cabral, left, with new .37mm Soviet cannon. A Cabral

PAIGC ZPU-4. A Cabral

A Tiger streams drogue chute at BA 12. J Nico

T-6 start-up at Nova Lamego. J Nico

66mm rockets on Fiat at BA12. J Nico

Tiger's CO gets send-off at BA12 in '68. J Santos

Sabre at Sal in transit to Guinea. Con e Silva

T-6 pilots and groundcrew at BA12. J Silva

QRA Fiat at BA12. J Silva

Tiger under tow at BA 12. FAP

80mm Soviet mortar. A Cabral

Mail Do-27 hit by SA-7. A Cabral

FAP helicopter. A Cabral

Pilot sends Xmas message from Guinea

PAIGC make propaganda film. A Cabral

Mosin-Nagant bolt-action rifle. A Cabral

ZPU-4 team on lookout for FAP. A Cabral

The feared ZPU-4. P Alegria

ZPU-4 taken from Fiat oblique nose camera. FAP

PAIGC canoe from Do27 recce cam. FAP

G-91 at OGMA with test Sidewinders. FAP

20mm AAA. A Cabral

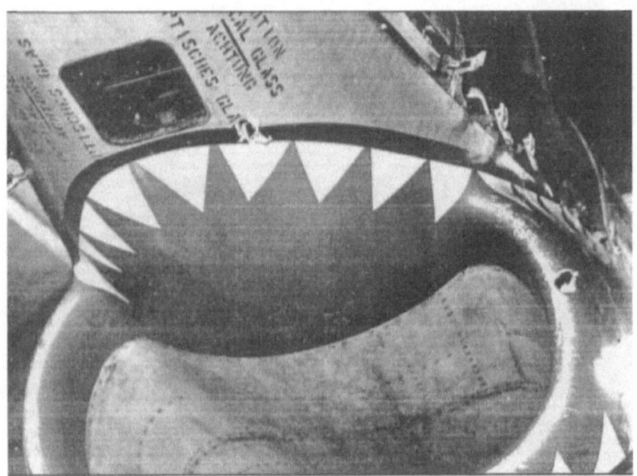

Fiat with PAIGC flak. FAP

The Pessoas after Miguel donated parachute to Tancos Para musem. M Pessoa

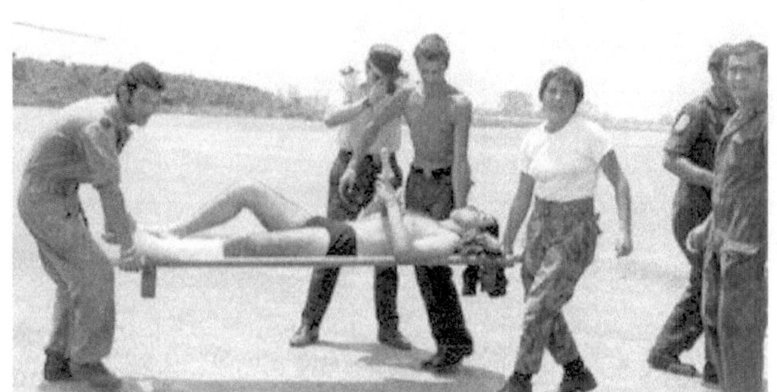

Miguel on stretcher which Giselda holds at BA12. M Pessoa

Fiat with dark olive green radiation paint. P Alegria

A Cabral second from right standing in Jardim da Estrela late 40s A Cabral

QRA Fiats return to BA 12. J Nico

PAIGC V POW Portugal. A Cabral

Max bomb load for BA12 Fiat. J Nico

Nice air-to-air of T-6 over water in Guinea. J Nico

Obusier 155m howitzer in action. A Cabral

18k-range Obusiers. A Cabral

A Luta Continua, the struggle continues! The rallying cry of FRELIMO independence fighters. Or all roads lead to Mueda

Mozambique was the final colony to rebel against Portuguese rule where Frente de Libertação de Moçambique (FRELIMO) launched its first raids in 1964. FRELIMO received bountiful support from newly independent Tanzania and its leader, Julius Nyerere, who allowed the independence group to use his country as a sanctuary. In 1964 Zambia and Malawi also gained independence adding to a climate favouring insurgencies into Mozambique.

The Portuguese territory has six frontiers and is around 1,800 kms long and about twice the size of California. FRELIMO leader Eduardo Mondlane had been educated in South Africa and Lisbon where he met several fellow independence leaders such as Amílcar Cabral of Cape Verde and Agostinho Neto of Angola. He had been teaching anthropology at a US university in 1962 when Tanzanian President Julius Nyerere decided he should become FRELIMO leader to pacify various factions of the party who were living in Tanzania. Soon after being appointed as FRELIMO chief Mondlane sent the first batch of 250 volunteers to newly independent Algeria for military training.

As the Mozambican insurgency progressed FRELIMO sent its recruits to more efficient training based in Russia and China and built up a network of bases and training camps in southern Tanzania as springboards to attack Portuguese forces to the south. In anticipation of unrest, Portuguese air power in Mozambique was initially centred on Aérodromo Base 8 (AB 8) in Lourenço Marques, now Maputo, the capital in the south and a long way from the north of the country where the initial FRELIMO incursions occurred. But by 1965 Base Aérea 10 (BA 10) in Beira, the second city, was operational in the centre of the country, as well as AM 52 at Nampula, served by forward bases along the northern frontiers with Malawi and Tanzania.

As in Angola where Portugal created Formações Aéreas Voluntárias (FAV) voluntary squadrons, Mozambique saw FAV 301 created in Beira and FAV 302 in Lourenço Marques with a combined 74 civilian pilots. The two FAV squadrons operated a mixture of Piper Tripacers, Colts, Apaches, Super Cubs, De Havilland Chipmunks, Tiger Moths, Beechcraft Bonanzas, Cesna 140s and Austers. During 1963 another 12 FAVs were set up in the north of Mozambique to cover the sprawling colony more effectively. Because Portugal was already engaged in two other tough colonial rebellions in Angola and Guinea-Bissau it was late to respond to need for a more robust FAP in Mozambique and the FAV voluntary squadrons, to some extent, plugged a gap in air-cover, especially observing and monitoring insurgent activity.

3 FAV pilots by Tiger Moth. J Costa

The first FAP aircraft with any significant attack capacity to arrive in Mozambique were two Lockheed PV-2 Harpoons arrived in 1962 in Beira and would become operational in the new Esquadra 101 a year later. Esq 101 had its first fatal accident in February 1963 when serial 4617 hit a power pylon on a low-level reconnaissance mission near the Mavuzi Dam. A power line became entangled on the Harpoon's starboard propeller, causing the plane to crash and explode, killing its pilot and five crew. But two other crewmen were miraculously pulled from the burning wreckage. The PV-2 was the sole aircraft in Esquadra 101 to use the F24 aerial camera and a replacement camera would be installed in another Harpoon several months later.

Esquadra 101 received its eighth and final PV-2 in May 1965 and a few months later the squadron was bolstered with 10 T-6Gs. The ageing Harpoons had been used since 1964 mainly on reconnaissance missions along FRELIMO infiltration routes across the Malawi border working with 24 T-6Gs assigned to forward airfields in the region. The PV-2s' five .50-caliber machines guns and 1365 kg bomb load were useful for attack missions against FRELIMO units, but the age of the WW2-era bomber coupled with maintenance issues continued to restrict its effectiveness and the squadron's Harpoon inventory would soon be cut to two aircraft.

The T-6Gs allocated to Mozambique were also starting to show their age and a once-abundant stock of spare parts and engines had run out. By 1967 all the Mozambican T-6Gs had had their rear cockpit instruments cannibalised to replace the front ones and a more potent and reliable replacement for both the T-6G and Harpoon would soon arrive in Mozambique: the Fiat G 91 medium attack jet. But the T6 continued until the end of the war with a peak of 47 aircraft in 1967. As FRELIMO never acquired much heavy AAA and only got SA-7 portable heat-seeking missiles from the Soviet Union in 1973 towards the end of the war, the T-6G remained useful to the FAP with its armament options of two Matra LR 361 canisters with 36 SNEB T/144 37mm rockets, 150kg bomb load or 80kg napalm canisters.

There were always around 30 of the converted trainers in the Mozambican skies in action until the end of the war in 1974. But the remaining Harpoons were transferred to Angola in 1967 because they were too difficult to maintain in Mozambique.

In a parallel insurgency in Angola the FAP had developed a helicopter gunship with an MG-151 20mm canon fitted to the Alouette 3 by 1965 after experimenting with various machine guns. A sole Alouette 2 had been sent from Esquadra 94 in Angola to Nampula in 1966 but the more powerful Alouette 3 did not arrive in Mozambique until October that year when six machines were sent to Esquadra 503 at

Alouette 3 refuelling in northern Mozambique. FAP

AB 5 in Nacala. In Angola the Alouette 3 gunships were used to cover troop insertions by other helicopters but in Mozambique they were initially used in operations with PV-2s, T-6Gs and Noratlas and Dakotas to insert paratroops.

The Esquadra 503 machines proved to be extremely useful in the remote areas of Mueda and Niassa where there were always high levels of FRELIMO activity. The FAP aircrew devised a system for hot refuelling of the Alouette 3 in high-tempo combat mission and could refuel a helicopter in less than eight minutes, cutting the ground time and returning it to the air. The FAP Alouette 3 fitted with MG-151 known as *tuberåo,* or shark, in Mozambique.

By 1966 the FAP's ageing Harpoons were facing severe maintenance issues and it became obvious that a more potent and reliable replacement was needed for the American bombers in their primary role of CAS of Portuguese troops trying to counter more frequent and damaging FRELIMO incursions into the north of Mozambique. But it would be another two years until the Harpoon replacement appeared in the skies, in the form of Fiat G 91s.

A typical and potentially hazardous FAP mission during 1967 in northern Mozambique was on 4 October when Flight Sergeants Gabriel Cavaleiro and Eiró Gomes in T-6Gs went on an armed reconnaissance to a location between Vila and Cabral, about 50kms from the Tanzanian border. They went to different spots where FRELIMO movement had been reported. Gomes came under heavy AAA tracer fire on a hill in a heavily wooded area. Cavaleiro went back to the source of the AAA and dropped his two 50kg and six 15kg bombs in salvo then the pair returned home.

T-6 in north. J Vera

In a follow-up sorties on 22 October Flight Lieutenant Manuel Malaquias was sent from the AM62 Marrupa forward airfield in a T-6G with Flight Sergeant Eiró Gomes and Flight Second-lieutenant Relego, also in T-6Gs, to the same location to evaluate if a joint Army operation was needed to destroy the FRELIMO AAA position. Lieutenant Relego had recently arrived in Mozambique after basic training in Portugal so he was ordered to stay above the other T-6Gs when they went to probe the suspected AAA position.

Lieutenant Malaquias said over the RT he was going to fly over the hill where he believed enemy fire had come from and told the other pilots to look for AAA and if the guerrillas opened fire, to bomb the spot. The other T-6Gs circled at different heights to get better views and the AAA opened up on Malaquias who returned fire with his two machine guns. Suddenly Malaquias shouted on the RT *Fui antingido! Nossa Senhora me valha!* I'm hit. Our Lady save me!

The T6G went down in thick forest in a shower of foliage and dust but didn't explode. But the shear desperation in the young FAP officer's voice and seemingly valedictory RT comments left the two T-6G pilots fearing the worst. Flight Sergeant Gomes, as senior aviator, took command of the Texan pair which headed for Marrupa and when he came within VHF range, about 40kms, he requested a helicopter be prepared to recover Malaquias who would most likely be dead or severely wounded at best. The nearest Portuguese Army unit to the downed T6G pilot was over 50 kms away so ground troops would not arrive that day.

Flight Sergeant Valdemar Lobo, a helicopter pilot originally from Cape Verde, immediately decided to take an Alouette 3 with three Polícia Aérea (PA) air force police volunteers on the highly risky mission which would be accompanied by two T-6Gs armed with machines guns to cover the helicopter's approach and exit to and from the FRELIMO position. The three policemen were armed only with side-arms and a few

Al 3 over north. J Vera

grenades. The PA officers were only trained to guard airbases and had no combat experience. Gomes and Relego, the two pilots who'd recently accompanied Lieutenant Malaquias' failed mission to destroy the insurgent AAA site, were too traumatised to show the other pilots so Flight Sergeant Borges Ferreira and Flight Sergeant Baguinho were the T-6G pilots on the mission to recover the lieutenant alive or his body. Both pilots were 21-year-old rookies with no combat experience. But when the Alouette 3 and T6Gs were near the mountainous area of deep forest.

Flight Sergeant Gomes came on to the helicopter's HF radio to guide them to the precise location of the downed T-6G less than two hours after Lieutenant Malaquias had been shot down. It took Flight Sergeant Lobo a few minutes to locate the T-6G, which had fallen between two large trees and had its right wing broken. The landing of the Alouette 3 for Flight Sergeant Lobo was tricky between large cropped tree trunks in the shade, with no artificial horizon on that model of the French-made machine. Lieutenant Malaquias had not made any attempt to force land the plane and its undercarriage was retracted, an indication he would be severely injured or probably dead.

As the three PA officers were walking to the aircraft, for around 300m they could see people in huts looking at them and some muskets and other weapons were being pointed at the courageous FAP personnel who soon found the aircraft and its pilot, who was dead with his right arm severed by the AAA. Lieutenant Malaquias' body was carried back to the Alouette 3 which soon took off still covered by the two T-6G, which had seen no enemy activity during the five-minute recovery operation. It later transpired that the site was a regional FRELIMO training base where dozens of guerrillas lived and had three heavy AAA guns on the sides of a valley overlooking it for protection from FAP intrusions.

The three FAP pilots and Air Force Police officers had no idea why they had been allowed by the FRELIMO fighters to recover their dead comrade when their aircraft could have been quickly shot down. Had the FRELIMO group decided to call a brief truce to allow the dead airman to be recovered or were they just stunned at the audacity of the Alouette 3 landing in the middle of their stronghold and Lieutenant Malaquias's dignified extraction from the crashed aircraft and transfer to the waiting helicopter?

But a few days later FRELIMO would issue an English-language communique, and a Portuguese one, about the shooting down of the T-6G with accurate details of its pilot and his downed plane and its location. The squadron commander at BA 5, Flight Brigadier Moura de Carvalho, wanted to discipline Flight Sergeant Lobo for endangering lives and equipment and one of the police officers involved in the recovery of Lieutenant Malaquias is still convinced that Lobo spent five days in military detention.

A fortnight before his doomed mission Lieutenant Malaquias had told his wife Fernanda that he was not long for this world and would soon be dead and buried. His wife suggested he went to the base medical officer but Lieutenant Malaquias declined for fear of being grounded. On his final T-6G flight, as he nearly always did when going on an operation, he had flown low over the family house near the Marrupa base, where his one-year-old daughter Carla lived with Fernanda.

About a year after the doomed Lieutenant Malaquias's daring recovery, his FAP comrades were advised that a FRELIMO prisoner was being interrogated at a nearby army base. One of Lieutenant Malaquias's closest friends, Flight Lieutenant Mira Godinho, felt an immediate urge to go the interrogation to see the FRELIMO fighter.

But by the time Godinho got to the building where the independence fighter was being questioned, his initial anger had subsided and the FAP pilot felt sympathy for the African on the other side of the Mozambican conflict and urged that he was not mistreated. Godinho handed over cigarettes and a bottle of Coke for the FRELIMO soldier.

Born in the skies of Turin with baptisms of fire over Lusophone Africa

In the September 1968 the FAP got permission to create its first jet squadron in Mozambique with Fiat G-91s supplied by Germany, which had already provided the same jets for Esquadra 121, Tigers, in Guinea. The new Fiat squadron was called Esquadra 502, *Jaguares* Jaguars and in late 1968 Flight Lieutenant Rui Matos André flew FAP G-91 serial 5431 in several test and training flights from Beira (BA 10) and on 30 December Flight Captain Fernando Fernandes in 4404 was the second Fiat in the air. The maiden flight of a pair of Fiat's over the skies of Mozambique was from the same base in Beira on 30 December 1968, to show residents in Mozambique's second city, and probably some FRELIMO activists, that Portugal had fast jet bombers to create aviation fires in areas hostile to the colonial power.

In May 1969 two Esquadra 502 Fiats were deployed to AB 6 at Nova Freixo and carried out various planned attack missions and a month later other Esquadra 502 G-91s operating from Beira attacked FRELIMO positions in the north with bombs and six 0.50 cal Brownings. From November 1968 to June 1969 Flight Lieutenant Matos Andre flew 52 hours in the eight new Fiats with over 13 hours in June, the peak G-91 deployment of the war in Mozambique.

In July the six Esquadra 502 G-91s attacked various FRELIMO sites as part of *Operaćāo Pesquisa* with 50kg, 100 kg and 350 litre general purpose bombs but during these missions tragically lost its CO, Flight Capitan Fernando Fernandes, in a Fiat, and Flight Lieutenant Matos Andre, in a T-6G , on the same day. Lieutenant Andre like nearly all FAP pilots was qualified for more than one type because there was always an acute shortage of pilots during the colonial wars. Around 300 pilots were available during the long insurgencies in the three colonies and they also had to fulfil missions in Portugal and for NATO. The two pilots had been the first to fly the Fiats in Mozambique a few months earlier and were among the FAP's most experienced aviators in Africa.

The Esq 502 Fiats flew 22 missions in July and another 27 the following month that were either armed reconnaissance or ground attack on FRELIMO positions and some assistance came from T6-Gs and the sole PV-2 Harpoon available. From September the eight G-91s were based at AB 6 Nova Freixo and Vila Cabral AM 61 for CAS operations in Niassa. The small Vila Cabral base, however, did not have the infrastructure to support more than two Fiats. In November 1969 Esquadra 502's jets worked from the larger AB 6 to attack FRELIMO on the the Miandica high-plane in 21 attacks with machine guns and rockets.

Esq 502 Fiats at AB6. R Barros

Gordian Knot of 1970, which would prove to be the largest Portuguese military offensive undertaken in the trio of African theatres, Guinea, Angola and Mozambique, was centred on the Mueda (AM 51) airbase where the only significant infrastructure and even that had many shortcomings with dilapidated buildings linked by a tar road that were always covered with dust from a local Army base. A crude sign was nailed to a pine tree in the middle of the Mueda FAP outpost that read:"Welcome to Mueda. Here we work, fight and die".

Since 1970 Portugal's top military commander was General Kaulza de Arriaga, who had different notions on how to tackle the FRELIMO insurgents. Instead of constant Army pressure with patrols and aviation support, he envisaged a large conventional sweep of Capo Delgado province with thousands of troops supported by artillery and the FAP. This was a counterinsurgency theory that had been abandoned by most generals in Portugal, as well as in Rhodesia and South Africa in their own insurgencies and bush wars. Gordian Knot was almost entirely devised by General Arriaga and was relatively straightforward, although a lot of adjustments had to be made because of the tricky terrains.

The FAP Mueda base was at 2,789 ft and needed another 1,200 ft runway for fully armed and fuelled Fiat G-91 to take off. The main rivers in the Gordian Knot operating zone held water all year and some could become formidable barriers to advancing soldiers. So helicopter insertion was going to be pivotal to success in driving FRELIMO from the area. Alouette 3 troop insertions in the area were difficult and unpredictably dangerous. They were normally heralded by Fiat bomb attack by Esquadra 502 Jaguars with the 454kg maximum load. The G-91's bombs would clear an LZ in the brambles.

Gordian Knot defined the battlefield around a central nucleus of villages which would be surrounded by Portuguese forces, backed by combat engineers and aviation resources.

There were an estimated 2,500 FRELIMO fighters in the area with 20,000 locals who were mainly controlled by the guerillas. General Arriaga assembled a force of 8,000 men and another 2,000 for logistic support to sweep FRELIMO from its wilderness stronghold.In parallel to Gordian Knot the FAP planned an autonomous operation called Sanctuary with separate missions against FRELIMO targets with Alouette 3s.

The Mueda base flight-line was packed with four Fiat G-91s, four T-6G, seven Alouette 3, one C-47 Dakotas, two Noratlas and three DO-27s. From 25 June 1970 the FAP unveiled successive raids on FRELIMO base Lúrio as a diversionary target from three real targets. The entire Gordian Knot period saw air operations impacted by weather conditions, particularly morning fog.

But the Fiats and T-6Gs managed to fly in the critical periods over the five-week operation. On 22 July the Fiats and T-6Gs left Mueda to provide fire support along the northern route between Mueda and Sagal with maximum bomb loads destroying FRELIMO targets.

Al 3s and a Do-27 at Mueda. J Vera

These FAP missions also identified guerrillas who had fled the Gordian Knot kill-zone. FRELIMO moved its units from Cabo Delgado province to Tete nearer to Rhodesia but Portuguese forces were now overextended and unable to prevent FRELIMO raids, especially after Rhodesian guerrillas began sharing bases with FRELIMO. And Portuguese leader Marcelo Caetano was unhappy at the soaring financial and military costs of massive operations that had inadvertently opened a new front with the rebels in Mozambique. Caetano had taken power in 1968 after dictator Salazar had a mild stroke in his deckchair.

Into 1970 the Esquadra 5O2 G-91s continued a cocktail of planned attack and armed econnaissance sorties against various FRELIMO targets in northern Mozambique but because the FAP still had an acute lack of bombing capacity with only about a dozen T-6Gs available and the final Lockheed Harpoon had been sent to Angola. It was decided to create a second Fiat squadron designated Escorpiões (Scorpions) Esquadra 702. FRE-LIMO was bolstering its support and fighters in Tete province after being forcibly ejected from Cabo Delgado in the Gordian Knot offensive. Valuable experience in maintaining experience advanced aircraft with more sophisticated avionics like the Fiat had been gained in Mozambique so an expansion of the fleet of the Italian-made plane was a logical move.

In July the first Esquadra 702 Fiats arrived by ship to Beira and were assembled at the local BA 10 and eight jets began training at Beira and the locality as their final destination of Tete AB 7 was still being upgraded. Tete had no hangar for the G-91s and the base would have a climate-controlled storage unit for the delicate electronics of the Fiat. Also the Tete region, next to the Zambian frontier, was effectively a wilderness with no navigational aids or radios to cover the operating zone of AB 7 and its forward airfields of Furancungo (AM 71), Mutarara (AM 73) and Chicoa (AM 72). It took until January 1971 for the new Fiat squadron to arrive in Tete when it began reconnaissance missions.

Esq 702 Fiat. I Strange

In the meantime the Mueda base had had its main runway closed to fully loaded Fiats from Esquadra 502 Jaguars, which began using the civil airport at Porto Amelia in spite of this airfield not having a long enough runway. The airfield was located on a high promontory overlooking the Indian Ocean and at the northern end of the runway lay the slim entrance to the largest deep-water harbour in the world. A three-Fiat detachment was started with pilot rotation from Nampula every fortnight. Fire support, armed reconnaissance and destruction of FRELIMO positions were the primary sorties for the Esquadra 502 G-91s in Cabo Delgado provinces. Destruction of enemy concentrations was undertaken in FAP-designated free-fire zones Esquadra 502 established via coordination with ground forces commanders.

Between April and September 1971 new Scorpions and battle-hardened Jaguars Fiats flew 650 missions using a large amount of munitions resulting in very low magazine stocks, especially bombs and fuzes, which reduced the number of attack sorties until the end of 1971. FRELIMO had returned to the fray after Gordian Knot with a new energy to attack Portuguese targets. The Fiats were in action in October 1971 against FRELIMO columns marching south from Tanzania and in one incident a T-6G pilot saw a large enemy group and confirmed its heading and location with several low passes. Airborne G-91s from Porto Amelia were sent to the area and killed many of the guerrillas in several strafing passes with the 0.50 machine guns. FRELIMO was becoming very concerned over the dominance of airpower in its plan to topple Portuguese rule of the colony.

However, the munitions shortage persisted for the FAP, which flew only 18 Fiat missions from Tete and 67 from Nacala in the first three months of 1972. After Portugal's close ally apartheid-era South Africa stepped into supply the shortfall of fuzes and bombs, which still weren't enough to dislodge FRELIMO from the Maconde Plateau. The insurgents had returned there and to the Gordian Knot former killing zone, a huge area with luxuriant foliage and tricky terrain. For the FAP a typical mission here was when an Esquadra 502 Fiat was hit by small arms fire 60 miles south of Mueda. It was the first such incident of a jet being hit by a rifle and interpreted as a sign that FRELIMO was starting to challenge Portuguese airpower. Another two Fiats from Esquadra 502 had to land next to the Tanzanian frontier when running low on fuel after searching for a missing T-6G that had seemingly been hit by AAA fire from Tanzanian territory.

Weather had been severe in the region and this probably led to the Fiat pair's fuel warning lights flashing. And lightning had struck one of the Fiats, which led to lack of power for radio navigation aids. The jets landed in marginal weather conditions and one had a flameout on finals. The two Fiat squadrons had their different missions dictated by terrain and the nature of local FRELIMO operations so in Tete the Esquadra 702 Scorpions mainly undertook reconnaissance on FRELIMO incursions to establish the group's behaviour and rationale. After the direction of the raid was established ground force missions of heli-borne assault would be used to annihilate the guerillas.

In Cabo Delgado Esquadra 502 Jaguars worked to stymie a well-established FRELIMO incursion strategy from Tanzania so sorties were nearly always armed reconnaissance or planned attack. These Fiat sorties were hampered by a lack of 2.75-inch rocket rails because this armament option with anti-personnel warheads were the preferred ordinance for planned attack against insurgents hiding in the grass. To try to compensate for this shortfall the Esg 502 Jaguars experimented with attaching 50k bombs to the rocket rails so the Fiats would not lack firepower on these missions.

But it transpired that the arming vanes on the bomb fuzes scored the Fiat's fuselage and wings so this was soon prohibited. Both jet squadrons had high levels of Fiat availability in 1972 with an average 200 hours a month per squadron. This was achieved in spite of the squadrons lacking six pilots between them and as the workload depended on the available Fiat pilots most literally

Fiat landing AB6. R Barros

lived in the aircraft at this point to fly missions purely in the vast north to destroy FRELIMO cadres and their bases. Portuguese ground troops also needed fire support from the Fiats in a timely manner and the FAP nearly aways delivered. Into 1973 FAP operations against FRELIMO became a serious threat to the guerrillas and their attempt to advance from their remote northern strongholds. FRELIMO decided to deploy more AAA and the 14.5mm quad-barrelled ZPU-4 made its debut in FRELIMO's stronghold zone where Gordian Knot had been unleashed in 1970. But moving the heavy ZPU-4 over well-policed terrain proved virtually impossible for FRELIMO.

There were some worries that the Mozambican insurgents would acquire the SA-7 surface-to-air missile that had recently appeared in Guinea-Bissau and downed several FAP planes including a Fiat. The PAIGC were the first non-regular troops to be trusted with the Soviet-made SA-7, whose presence would soon drastically restrict bombing to above 8,000 ft in Guinea. On 15 March 1973 Esquadra 502 lost Fiat G-91 5429 flown by Flight Lieutenant Emilio Lourenço when a defective fuse exploded a 50kg bomb over Tete. It was the second fatal Fiat crash for the squadron after the 1969 loss of Flight Capt Fernando Fernandes.

Of the 40 Fiats acquired in 1967 from Germany the FAP now had 35, of which 10 were at BA 12 in Guinea, 15 in Nacala and Tete in Mozambique and another 10 in Portugal used for pilot training and at OGMA, the main maintenance centre near Lisbon. There was a pressing need to strengthen the Fiat squadrons in Guinea and Mozambique but it had been decided by the FAP's Chief of Staff that there should be only 35 Fiat-qualified pilots in Africa to operate the 25 jets assigned to Guinea and Mozambique and these numbers would not be increased.

FRELIMO 37mm AAA. G Cavaleiro

Consequently the FAP campaigns in Guinea, against the highly trained and effective PAIGC, and Mozambique, against an increasingly belligerent FRELIMO, now rested on a handful of Fiats and their pilots to bomb, machine gun and rocket the African independence group. Esq 502 managed to find three Fiat-qualified staff officers to fly its jets, which proved to be a significant help. In June 1973 a Fiat failed to deploy its drogue chute on landing at Beira and overshot the runway. Soon after this structural cracks associated with firing the six 0.50 calibre guns on the G-91 were found, which impacted on high usage rates as all the Mozambican Fiats needed inspections.

Esquadra 502, the Jaguars, started to encounter heavy AAA when attacking the main FRELIMO bases near the border with Tanzania and developed new attack profiles to reduce risks with the Fiats arriving at dawn when the half-light would reveal AAA firing at them. The FAP tactic was refined to attack the gun emplacements with full bomb load and the sun rising behind them to blind the FRELIMO gunners. FAP flyers soon dubbed this tactic the "hot breakfast". For the Fiat pilots the "heat" of the mission happened in their own takeoff roll with a full fuel and bomb capacity. Porto Amelia's 6,000 ft runway would mean the jets reached rotation speed in the final 100 ft of tarmac.

Mueda stayed open to the G-91s but it was not suited for heavy use so pilots continued to land, refuel and rearm when conditions allowed. In May 1973 a Fiat using Mueda was hit by three 14.5mm bullets, a clear sign FRELIMO was reinforcing AAA defences again. In other areas of its weapons inventory FRELIMO acquired Katyusha 122mm rockets by June 1973 and the Mueda base became the preferred target for these Soviet-made rockets that were launched from cover of dense grass at up to 10 kilometres. The first attacks on besieged Mueda, which also had a Portuguese Army outpost, were not very successful but the guerrillas' aim would eventually get better!

The FAP pilot shortage continued and at the end of 1973 there were a mere 11 pilots for the two Fiat squadrons in Mozambique. Five more aviators were needed urgently to keep FRE-LIMO at bay but the number of G-91 flying hours had dropped to the 1967 level when they first started working to stymie the insurgency in

Fiat landing Mueda. FAP

the north. Maintenance was also an issue on the jets, which were obviously already second-hand when acquired from West Germany. A support team from OGMA was dispatched to try to improve the front-line servicing of the Fiats in Mozambique.

But FRELIMO was getting bolder and stronger and beginning to operate more outside Cabo Delgado and Tete provinces. FRELIMO would often appear in small patrols now relatively far south and generate anxiety in the local populations, who didn't support them. In 1973 the Esquadra 702 Scorpion Fiats in Tete made use of a Fairchild K-20 aerial camera fitted to a napalm canister for reconnaissance missions at 15,000 ft along both sides of the Zambian border to avoid the new SA-7 and any other ground fire.

Zambia had become independent in 1964 and President Kenneth Kaunda supported FRELIMO and in March 1973 the Fiat's overhead reconnaissance revealed depots used by the independence fighters to supply Tete in Mozambique. The FAP photography in early March also showed large numbers of FRELIMO troops massing for a raid just outside Gago Coutinho in Tete. On March 3 two Esq 702 Fiats were launched from AB 7 Tete to destroy the FRELIMO force with maximum bomb load before it had a chance to attack the Gago Coutinho base. In the early afternoon the FAP jets found their target, causing heavy losses and forcing the surviving FRELIMO troops back into Zambia.

In September an Alouette 3 on another reconnaissance sortie spotted a FRELIMO depot hidden in particularly difficult terrain. The guerrillas had obviously heard the noisy helicopter and knew they'd been seen by the FAP. They stayed put, feeling secure against the lone unarmed Alouette, which in the meantime contacted Tete to call up AB 7 to call an attack by two Fiats, which could tackle the inhospitable terrain and AAA and destroyed the enemy site. But in general it was proving difficult to target FRELIMO supply lines coming through Zambia into Tete as they were now defended by 14.5mm AAA, which proved especially lethal to the FAP Dorniers connecting the remote bases on liaison sorties and supplies and the voluntary FAV planes and pilots with both supplies and vital mail.

In 1973 alone FRELIMO gunners managed to hit 11 DO-27s, seven Fiats, four Dakotas, five Noratlas, three T-6G and ten Alouette 3s, resulting in the death of a pilot and two crew. Towards the end of 1973 the FAP acquired airborne infrared technology that was fitted to a Dakota to detect insurgents hiding in the deep foliage so some FRELIMO bases were eliminated by loitering G-91s bombing them. This destruction of bases and killing of its cadres sparked a recruitment crisis for the liberation fighters, FRELIMO Central Committee member Joaquim Chissano said after the war. Chissano served as Mozambique's second president from 1986 to 2005.

Due to the likelihood of imminent FRELIMO possession of SA-7, known to Portuguese aviators by its Russian name Strela, Mozambique's Fiats were now limited to planned attacks with the top bomb load delivered in a single pass from 8,000 ft and a 45-degree angle with the sun at the pilot's back. The new missile could be confused by the sun and still had no head-on acquisition capacity. These measures countered the SA-7 threat to Fiats in the African theatre and didn't reduce the FAP's attack sorties.

FRELIMO trains all guns on Mueda

Mueda AM 51was the most strategically important – and most attacked – FAP base in northern Mozambique throughout the war and the most devastating was on 20 January 1974 when a barrage of 122mm Katyusha rockets set the aviation fuel tanks on fire. In 1966 FRELIMO had used 60mm Chinese mortars near the end of runway 16 and damaged a T-6G and helicopter. Afterwards the vegetation was cleared for a 40mm cannon and later 20mm AAA to fire high-volume bullets horizontally. FRELIMO then always attacked the vulnerable base from the north with 82mm mortars and later the 122m Soviet Katyusha, with a maximum 3,000 meters range.

To protect its precious aircraft, and fuel supplies, over the years concrete revetments were installed next to the flight line and a protected fuel trench system for about 1,500 200-litre drums of JP-4 jet fuel. Obviously Mueda's protected fuel facilities were a coveted target for FRELIMO and Portugal's local PIDE Inspector Casimiro Monteiro had told the base commander José Queiroga on Christmas Eve that FRELIMO had intended to launch a major assault on the base that very night but the guerrillas had to cancel the operation as there weren't enough porters to transport the 122mm rockets.

The expected date for the delayed Mueda attack was now between 16 and 24 January so an Alouette 3 gunship made a daily armed reconnaissance along the cleared runway approaches to the base and on 19 January all appeared normal but bad weather brought thunder and lightning and FAP communications were affected, potentially isolating AM 51.

FRELIMO used the storm to set up their rockets during the night and at around 04.30 unleashed a 20-minute barrage with four 122m launchers from a ravine below Mueda and by chance hit the fuel pits, sparking a blaze that consumed 300,000 litres of fuel. Smoke and flames rose in columns but fortunately the brisk wind took most of the smoke away from the airfield where Flight Major Vaz Afonso, with rockets still falling around him, taxied his Fiat to the runway and took off with four 50kg bombs.

Fiats scramble in Mueda raid. FAP

Seconds later a rocket hit the runway where he had started his takeoff. The rest of the Mueda Fiats were soon in the air as all FAP personnel on the base knew their respective jobs after the alarm had sounded. An Alouette 3 rose vertically to look for the FRELIMO firebase and Vaz Afonso's G-91 said on the RT the enemy location was at 160 degrees and eight kilometres from Mueda and that there were 82mm mortars about 3 kilometres away. The FRELIMO 82mm rocket team were destroyed in around 20 minutes by the Fiats.

The first appearance of the SA-7 missile in Mozambique was on 10 April 1974 in a FAP raid in Tete province where there was no consequence. But on 20 April two Rhodesian Air Force Trojans looking for a FRELIMO base were shot down by the Soviet-supplied compact weapon that had virtually ended Portuguese air supremacy in Guinea in 1973. Even though the Carnation Revolution had occurred in April 1974, FRELIMO remained stalemated in northern Mozambique and decided to use the ceasefire with the new Portuguese Army-led government to expand its presence by force and get a bigger control of the country as it would probably be defeated in the mooted referendum.

For an unknown rationale the new military chiefs in Lisbon after the virtually bloodless Army coup by war-weary leftist junior officers decided it was a good moment for military attachés accredited to Portugal to visit Mozambique's combat zone. Some seven senior officers then arrived at Beira and the FAP took them on a VIP Dakota called "Silver Arrow" to Nampula then Mueda where the base commander briefed the visitors on FAP operations and the advent of the SA-7, which the Fiat G-91s always flew at over 10,000 ft to avoid.

The FAP Dakota then landed at Nangade, a besieged Portuguese outpost heavily protected by rapid-firing guns to fend off FRELIMO attacks which still occurred. A week previously FRELIMO 122m rockets were unleashed on Nangade before a sole G-91 took out the rockets in a single bombing. After a briefing at Nangade everyone boarded for the return flight to Nampula with rain starting and cumulonimbus clouds forecast on the route near Mueda and most of the enemy-held parts of the Maconde Plateau.

A safe altitude of 10,000 ft was chosen above the 1,500 terrain below so the Dakota needed to reach 11,500 ft to be safe. Flight Captain José Assunção had problems on the weather side with driving rain and lightning and turned eastward to find clearer weather but conditions were worse still and the Dakota failed to get over the clouds or even the 11,500 ft safety altitude. Unfortunately Capt Assunção, his crew and illustrious passengers were now tempting bait for the multiple SA-7s in and around the main FRELIMO base.

The heat-seeking missile hit the right engine of the FAP Dakota and shattered a window near to the German attaché, who went into shock after the explosion that rocked the aircraft violently. The captain told the flight engineer to cut the right engine's fuel

FAP Dakota. I Strange

and ignition and continued to fly on the working one and turned towards Mueda to request an emergency landing. Speed was cut to 100 knots and it was established there were no injuries to the passengers or crew. But due to bad weather the Mueda tower directed the Dakota to land at a small packed-earth airfield at Nacatari.

There were no navigational beacons for Nacatari and its 1,300 ft runway so Capt Assunção managed to line up with the runway using the Mueda beacon for compass fix and made a 270- degree turn, keeping the damaged engine on the outside of the manoeuvre. The vibrations heightened with each turn and many passengers believed death was imminent. The Dakota's airspeed bled to 65 knots on the 10 degree flaps the pilot opted for and on landing the working engine was shut down to prevent a fire.

The pilot chose to land on grass to the right of the runway as it would provide better braking traction and the missile-afflicted aircraft spun left in an almost total reverse of direction. The passengers all abandoned the Dakota quickly and were taken to Nampula first in a flight of Alouette 3s and then a Noratlas transport.

Extra images for Mozambique section

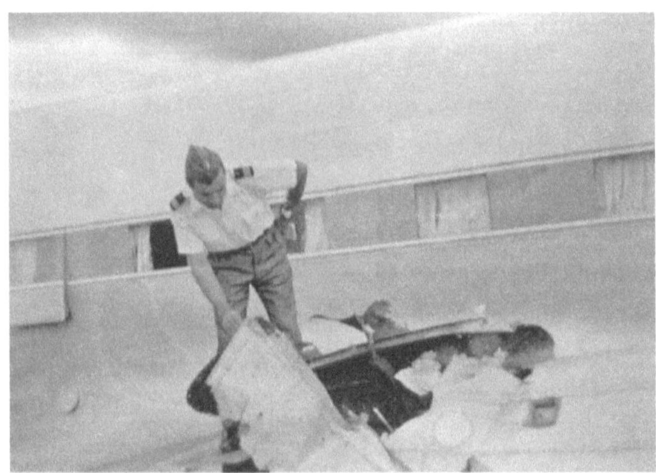

Dakota capt inspects missile damage. FAP

Silver Arrow immediately after landing. FAP

The first Fiat flier in Mozambique Rui Matos André taking to local FAP brass in 68. FAP

Pair of Jaguars Fiats at BA6. R Barros

G-91 trio at Nampula in 70. FAP

Fiat with bombs after BA6 take-off accident. R Barros

T-6 and Do-27 flightlines at Nampula. J Vera

Jaguars Fiat with T-6 and Do-27 at BA6. R Barros

Portuguese Army convoy in north. I Lippman

Mixed FRELIMO in Lourenço Marques in 74. I Lippman

Al 3 troop carriers and gunship in north. J Vera

*Rare Harpoon at Mueda in 69 with Noratlas, T-6s and Do-27
taking off. J Vera*

*Bold FRELIMO patrol in Lourenço Marques (Maputo) in 74. I
Lippman.*

T-6 with rockets covers Al 3 medevac. I Lippman

Al 3 troop insertion after Fiat bombing. I Lippman

The besieged Mueda base during enlargement in 1970. FAP

Traumatised Portuguese soldier enters Al 3. I Lippman

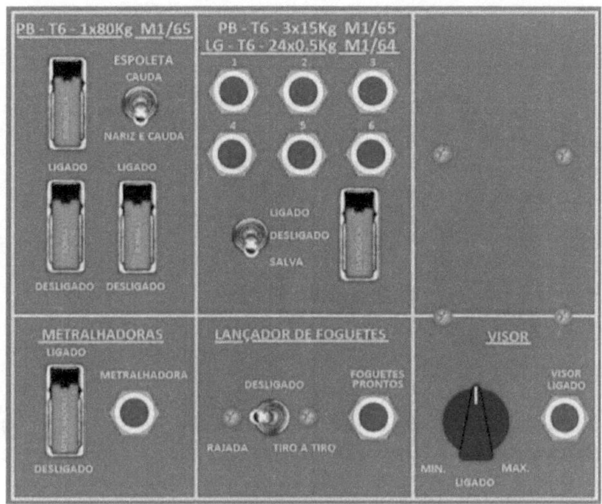

T-6 weapons panel from Museu do Ar, Sintra. C Barrett

Esq 93 Thunderjet refuels at Beira during 66 Crisis. FAP

*Valdemar Lobo, left, pilot in Malaquias recovery who later be-
came head pilot of TACV Cape Verde state carrier. G Cavaleiro*

*Lt Malaquias holding helmet with Ramalho Eanes, who joined
the 74 MFA Army Coup and became President for 10 years !*

```
                    NIASSA PROVINCE
                WESTERN MILITARY REGION

    During the period from the 4th of August to the 29th of October
    FRELIMO forces killed at least 180 Portuguese soldiers, put out of
    action over a hundred more, shot down one plane, destroyed 15
    military vehicles, blew up a railway line, attacked three bases
    and captured a fourth.

    On the 31st of August FRELIMO guerrillas launched an attack against the
    Portuguese military post of MANIAMBA. After our attack of August 15th against
    that same post, the Portuguese forces had left and abandoned that zone. Some
    days later new enemy reinforcements arrived and occupied the post. On the
    31st our fighters attacked again and destroyed the huts where the Portuguese
    soldiers were sleeping, in a combined action of our artillery and infantry
    forces. As a result of the attack, many enemy soldiers were killed and others
    wounded (We do not however know the exact numbers)Those who survived ran away
    and refused to return to MANIAMBA. 10 days later a new enemy unit arrived and
    again occupied the post. This new unit is from the marines.

    On September 7th several guerrilla units (artillery and infantry) attacked the
    enemy post of NCOO. The barracks where the Portuguese soldiers were sleeping
    were destroyed. They could not answer our fire. 15 of the enemy were killed and
    many wounded.

    On the 22nd of October, at 3.30 pm, a Portuguese military aircraft was  shot
    down in NGAZELO. It was part of the Portuguese local air-force, which had been
    bombing the whole zone of Werrupa. Our fighters opened fire against these
    aircraft, three in all, shooting down one of them. Its identification  number
    was T 6 - G,52-8603, registration number, 1739. Our fighters captured the docu-
    ments of the pilot - LIEUTENANT MANUEL MALAQUIAS DE OLIVEIRA - and his pistol,
    no. 113202. The pilot himself was dead. The equipment of the aircraft, which
    included 6 machine guns,was captured but in the crash it had been damaged beyond
    repair.

    On the 12th of October FRELIMO guerrillas attacked the enemy camp of MACHOMANE.
    The Portuguese soldiers were on parade. They were attacked by surprise and suffered
    many casualties.

                                                                            13
```

FRELIMO statement about death of Lt Malaquias. G Cav-
aleiro

Lt Malaquias, first left, with Do-27 and rocket pod

At table from left to right FRELIMO leader Joaquim Chissano, Samora Machel and Oscar

Painting of infamous Mueda sign. F Serra.

Noratlas on Para drop in northern Mozambique. FAP

Ricardo Barros on break at BA6 with G-91 and 'elephant moun-
tain' in bakground. R Barros

T-6 in north, J Vera

Over Beira in 69 a flight of Noratlas.

Manuel 'Manecas' Aleixo brings Do-27 into AB6. C Aleixo

Puma at Nacala. M Silva

Fiat generates few Gs for Jaguars pilot over BA6 in 69. R Barros

Manecas Aleixo looping a T-6 over BA6 in 68. C Aleixo

Rhodesian AF Hawker Hunter at Tete. FAP

Al 3 troop drops after Fiat LZ clearance in '70. I Lippman

Rhodesia AF Trojans at Tete. FAP

Chopper approaching Mueda in mist. FAP

FAV 305 DH Chipmunk at Inhambane. P Santos

FAV ID of pilot.

T-6 of João de Sousa killed doing acrobatics.

FAV Piper Turbo Comanche with mail and supplies at Mueda.
in 68 J Vera

another view of Mueda. F Serra

Rare FAV Do-27 after tailwheel prang. M Silva

"to fly and serve" motto of FAV 202 in Lourenço Marques. B Silva

T-6 at Nacala. J Silva

Female fighters at FRELIMO HQ. I Lippman

Eduardo Mondlane on traditional instru-
ment. Was either killed by PIDE in '69 or
party rival. MSF

Jaguars Fiat. I Strange

From 1953 to '73 FAP operated 69 C-47s. I Strange

First G-91s and pilots at Lourenço Marques (Maputo). FAP

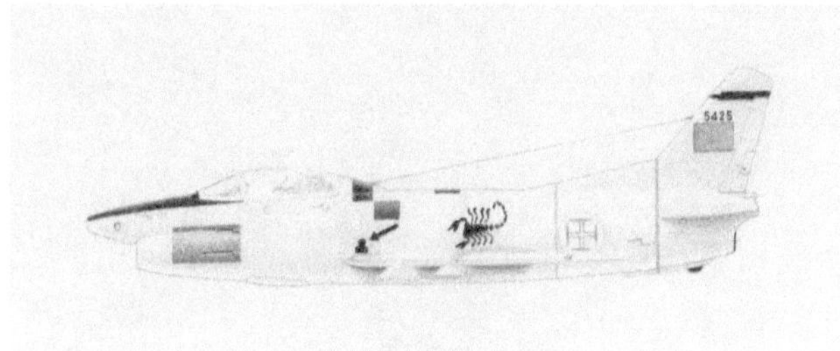

Jaguars Fiat. I Strange

The Portuguese Neptune in Arica

The Força Aérea Portuguesa (FAP) acquired 12 Lockheed P2V-5 Neptunes from the Royal Netherlands Navy from April 1960 over 12 months and the second-hand maritime patrol aircraft were assigned to Esquadra 61 at Base Aérea 6 at Montijo, near Lisbon, where the Lockheed PV-2 Harpoon had previously been operated. The Neptune squadron's main roles had been intended to be anti-submarine patrols and maritime patrols but armed insurrections in Portugal's African territories meant the P2V-5s were quickly dispatched to Africa. But diplomatic friction between Portugal and the US began in 1961 when the FAP sent a squadron of F-86F Sabres to Guinea-Bissau to attack independence fighters in the West African territory.

As the Sabres had been supplied under MDAP terms they should only be used to defend NATO's southwestern flank in Europe and the FAP F-86Fs returned to Portugal in 1964. Keen to avoid similar sensitivities with Washington, as well as NATO, over its Neptune fleet future deployments to Africa of the aircraft would be short-term detachments. Detachment 61 to Bissau, capital of Guinea-Bissau, during 1961 of two P2V-5s and their crews and a maintenance team was the first temporary deployment to Africa of the Neptunes.

The Neptune had 12 weapons hardpoints, which could carry bombs from 50 kg to 340 kg. The P2V-5 could carry anti-submarine weapons like torpedoes, depth charges and sea mines. Rocket launchers below the wings could take up to 16 2.25, 2.75 or 5in rockets. But there was no precision bomb-aiming system so only area targets could be attacked. Portugal had begun a guerrilla war in Guinea against the PAIGC and in January 1964 the FAP Neptunes were in action against the insurgents in Operation Trident.

A P2V-5 dropped two 50kg bombs on PAIGC canoes in support of Portuguese Army units in a mission also involving FAP T-6Gs. A FAP Auster had dropped leaflets to warn residents of the planned attack. The first night bombing by the Portuguese Neptunes occurred the same month targeting suspected PAIGC positions in the Cachil forest in Guinea using 50k bombs and on 29 February a follow-up operation took place in daylight.

In 1965 the PAIGC began building AAA defences in Cantanhez and two Neptunes were dispatched from Sal in Cape Verde to the Bissalanca base in Guinea, on 18 December making night raids using 325k bombs after a FAP C-47 had dropped magnesium flares to illuminate the night sky. The Neptune attacks took place over two consecutive nights but on the second night the PAIGC guns fell silent so the operation in Guinea was concluded.

The remaining African missions for the Neptune fleet were in Angola, where Detachment 62 was created in 1963 at BA 9, Luanda, and two aircraft undertook offshore and overland reconnaissance operations due to their long range. In November 1965, in response to the Beira crisis sparked by the then Rhodesian government's unilateral declaration of independence, the Portuguese government sent six Luanda-based F-84G Thunderjets, under the command of Flight Captain Fernando Moutinho, to Beira BA 10 in Mozambique where they remained until May 1966.

T-6 with Neptune in Operation Trident. P Alegria

At the same time two FAP Neptunes were sent to the same Mozambican base to monitor Royal Navy ships and the remaining four FAP Lockheed Harpoons from Esquadra 101. As Detachment 63 the P2V-5s began maritime reconnaissance in an area bounded by Save and Zambezi rivers extending 150 miles into the channel between Madagascar and Mozambique. At the peak of the Rhodesia crisis the pair of Neptunes never exceeded a monthly limit of 95 hours flying time. Detachment 63 ended in 1968 and the Neptunes returned to Portugal.

The final deployment to Portuguese Africa was in 1970 when Portugal invaded Republic of Guinea, which neighboured Guinea-Bissau, and backed the PAIGC rebels. A single Neptune accompanied a six-ship Portuguese Navy force over the 120-mile trip that took just over a day. The Portuguese operation was a partial failure but the Neptune performed its task well and prevented any hostile boats attacking the Portuguese.

As the Portuguese Neptunes were often used for SAS missions in Europe and Sal in Cape Verde they sometimes got called out to look for missing civilians in boats. But one of the more memorable occasions when the P2V-5 were called into action when based in Cape Verde in West Africa was on September 21, 1967, during the Nigerian Civil war. The then Flight Capt José Martins told *Aeroplane Monthly* recently that his Neptune got a call from the tower at Sal that a Meteor NF14 fighter en route from Portugal to Sal was 30 minutes overdue and its last reported position was "abeam of the Spanish Canaries".

The British-made jet, registered as G-ASLW, had been acquired by the fledgling state of Biafra, which had recently broken away from Nigeria and was building up its own air arm. Capt Martins said his Neptune left Sal at 09.30 to search an area northwest of Cape Verde but without spotting any ditched jets or signs of life. The search continued the next day and Dakar SAR centre in Senegal suggested the search was made on an axis between Sal and the Canaries on a 'creeping line' heading north.

The Neptune's navigator told Martins that it was time to begin the final leg of the 'creeping line'as they were running short on fuel after 10 hours in the air. Out of conscience Martins opted to have a final look to the east and on the last leg the Neptune's flight engineer shouted enthusiastically "I've seen smoke to our left". A small dinghy with the missing pilot on board was soon spotted.

The downed aviator was Dutchman Pieter Dezeeuw whose happiness surpassed that of the Portuguese SAR team! But the new mission for the Harpoon was not straightforward as a large lifeboat with capacity for 20 people now had dropped with the normal stiff north-easterly wind and associated swell. The Dutch pilot's location was first marked with ink and smoke bombs from the Neptune flying at 100ft. The lifeboat self-inflated on descent, touching down on the water totally inflated and had been dropped so the wind would carry it to the pilot, whom they saw climbing into the small boat and immediately jumping for joy!

The Dutch pilot needed to be picked up but there was no Portuguese Navy ship available so the Harpoon crew made an emergency VHF call, which was picked up by a Dutch freighter close by so the pilot was soon speaking his native tongue. By now the FAP SAR mission had lasted over 12 hours so the Neptune returned to its Sal base while a French Navy aircraft kept an eye on Pieter Dezeeuw in his lifeboat. The merchant ship collected the Dutch pilot and the FAP lifeboat and he was taken to the Sal base on arrival in Cape Verde later that day.

Dezeeuw spent around three days on Sal Island recovering and nearly always had a glass in his hand, Capt Martins said. The Meteor had left Faro in Portugal on its penultimate leg to Sal with a full load of fuel and only a radio compass to navigate. The pilot got confused several times by cloud shadows which he mistook for islands so had to climb and descend more than planned which wasted fuel. He eventually ran out about 90 miles north of Sal.

The Meteor did not have the usual Martin Baker seat so the pilot managed to exit the aircraft in the dark using a parachute. He said what impressed him most were the flying fishes jumping over him and had had very little hope of being found until he heard the FAP Neptune and made careful use of his remaining flares and smoke.

Dutch pilot with Neptune and crew at Sal. J Martins.

In the cruise. Con' e Silva

At Sal Airport in 69. Con' e Silva

Between Sal and Guinea. Con' e Silva

At BA12 in Guinea. Con' e Silva

Off the Algarve coast in Portugal. Con' e Silva

Over Sagres, Portugal. Con' e Silva

At Montijo in 69. FAP

Near Sal in 69. Con' e Silva

P Alegria

At Sal with Sabre. Con' e Silva

The Imperial Airline

In the late 1950s Portugal's military aviation supremos began developing a so-called imperial airline to serve the passenger and cargo requirements of its sprawling Empire that was mainly in Africa but still extended to Goa in India and East Timor in southeast Asia. The focus of the imperial airline concept was the appearance of a few Douglas C-54 Skymaster, Boeing C-97 Stratofreighter and Lockheed C-121 Constellation during WW2 and just after it.

As a WW2 neutral Portugal was fortunate to acquire, via internment, six B-24 Liberator heavy bombers in WW2 that allowed it to gain its first experience in flying and maintaining modern four-engined long-range aircraft that could be used in the transport role. Arguably the B-24 was the best WW2 bomber after it deployed in May 1943 in Europe after the Boing B-17 Flying Fortress had been the main US-made bomber used against Nazi Germany. The B-17, in the popular imagination at least, is often seen as the bomber that beat Hitler but most aviation historians rate it as average but with a great PR department. Most people have seen the WW2 documentary Memphis Belle or its 1990 Hollywood treatment. The B-24 could fly farther and faster than the B-17 and had a bigger bomb capacity. Portugal would acquire some B-17s in the 1950s but only deployed them in an SAR role.

By 1959 the FAP had created its Transporte Aéreo Militar (TAM) transport arm that had a dozen C-54s. In 1966 five SAR versions of the C-54 were added to the TAM fleet, meaning 18 aircraft were operating on the imperial airline, although the US demanded that the six SAR aircraft only operated in the North Atlantic so the imperial fleet was limited to 11 planes. And as the C-54 was a WW2 vintage machine it effectively took two days to fly the 10,500 km from Lisbon to Luanda with its 165-knot cruise speed. In the case of an emergency in its empire the C-54 would not be enough to send more troops and supplies so another solution would be needed by the FAP, which came in the welcome availability of the DC-6 Cloudmaster and its military version, the C-118 Liftmaster, both faster, larger and pressurised versions of the C-54.

The ex-Pan American World Airways DC-6s were put on a Lisbon, Luanda, Lourenço Marques (Maputo) route up to three times weekly for two years until maintenance issues meant never more than six aircraft were available.Portuguese flag flier TAP had moved to all-jet operation in 1967, after acquiring Boeing 707s, to be the first European carrier to be totally jet. In 1969 the FAP controversially ordered three 707s of its own. The Boeing-707 purchase was contested by many on the grounds of the expense in brand-new aircraft and training ground support teams. But once the Boeing 707-3F5Cs trio were delivered to the FAP in 1970 they enjoyed extremely high rates of use until the end of the war, with their mixed passenger and freight cabins and strengthened undercarriage. The DC-6 was only used on shorter routes to Guinea and Europe, with the Boeing 707 typically leaving Lisbon at 11.30 for Luanda and returning at 22.30 the same day. The imperial airline dream had been finally realised with the 707s saving about USD 11m in three years after the costs of using sea freight or DC-6s for the same military personnel and cargo.

TAM 707 at Lisbon. FAP

C-54 in Mozambique. M Silva

707 at BA4, Angola. FAP

C-54 at BA9. C Costa

C-54 at BA9. C Costa

TAM C-54s at Lisbon in 69. FAP

TAM 707 in Nacala. M Silva

The FAP Paranurse corp

The 1961 UPA attacks in northern Angola had proved that Portugal lacked the capacity to give prompt medical care to the wounded and there was a particular lacuna in evacuation from the battlefield. Initially it was thought male nurses in the Army could be turned into paranurses but soon it became clear that female nurses could well be more suited to the role, especially during the evacuation of wounded military personnel in the field. In socially conservative Portugal the notion of putting the gentler sex in harm's way was quite revolutionary and would need a great deal of groundwork if it were to come to fruition.

Originally Portuguese leader Salazar was concerned over the female nurses serving in all-male isolated environments but Portuguese military chiefs assured Salazar that all volunteers would be chosen from nursing colleges run by the Catholic Church and therefore imbued with robust morals. The sisters running the nursing schools got behind the plan with enthusiasm and were asked to award the distinctive green berets to their ex-students when the latter graduated from the military course.

On 6 June 1961 the first *Corpo de Enfermeiras Pára-quedistas* started with five officers and one sergeant. The students all had Maria as Christian name and so were known as the "six Marias". After graduating on 8 August after making the last of six qualifying parachute leaps the sisters awarded the berets to the "six Marias". In early 1973 South African war reporter Al Venter interviewed paranurse Maria Conceição Pais who had served three years in Guinea, the toughest and deadliest theatre by a long chalk for the Portuguese military in Africa.

Before joining the Corps she was a doctor's receptionist and had never been more than 50 kilometres from her home village in northern Portugal. Pais finished high school and said she felt unchallenged by life with the prospect of marrying a local and spending the rest of her days in a closed, parochial society and eventually dying within a day's walk of where she was born.

But when the opportunity arose when the colonial wars kicked off she enlisted swiftly with altruism probably a small part of her personal motivation at the time. Her subsequent war experiences and training produced a nurse with drive and character. She had been part of a highly professional team in Guinea whose dozen members led a difficult and often dangerous existence. One paranurse was killed in Guinea when her head was hit by the propeller of a Dornier during a medevac. Portugal had taken a bold step in creating the all-female Corps to ease its manpower shortage. During the 14 years the programme ran a total 48 paranurses graduated and all served in combat.

Five of 6 Marias after graduating.
FAP

Corporal Nuno Almeida, a FAP medical orderly who served in Guinea in 1972, has given dramatic accounts of some of his personal experiences in the back of helicopters working nearly exclusively with the female paranurses. He wrote them up in 2017 for a book on the elite medical team. He flew to Teixeiro Pinto to collect one of the elite African commando units had been in combat with a PAIGC patrol. The helicopter landed and Almeida prepared to grab a stretcher and step out but saw a very tall African soldier carrying his weapon in one hand and a typical Portuguese *saco de pão* (a drawstring cotton bread bag) in the other. Portuguese troops often took fresh bread and items like tinned tuna on patrols in the Guinean jungle that could last for several days.

The African elite soldier had entered the Alouette in what appeared to be a trance and sat in Almeida's usual seat in the rear where there were three forward-facing seats opposite three facing the other way. The apparently traumatised African soldier's rifle was stowed in a safe part of the Alouette and he sat on one of the rear seats with his bread bag on the next seat, which he seemed reluctant to hand over.

A paranurse was sitting next to the bread bag and after a few minutes started signalling to Almeida in the noisy machine if he knew what was in the bag because it stank. The nurse then carefully tried to open the bread bag's drawstring to see what was causing the very unpleasant odour and screamed so loudly she could be heard by Almeida and others over the background noise from the rotors and engine. It turned out that the African soldier, fighting for Portugal, had decapitated a PAIGC combatant he had killed in the recent engagement with the guerillas.

This gruesome action by the African soldier was in keeping with his own traditional beliefs that if he didn't decapitate someone he had killed in combat he would be haunted by that person in future. The consequence for the special forces soldier on arrival in Bissalanca was being diagnosed with a high fever on arrival on his medevac. Only one of the elite nurses died in Africa, Maria da Costa in Guinea by the propeller of a FAP Do-27 while on a mission.

Paranurses boarding JU-52 for training jump. FAP

Maria Reis. right, and Maria Arminda, kneeling, boarding with Paras in Angola in 61. FAP

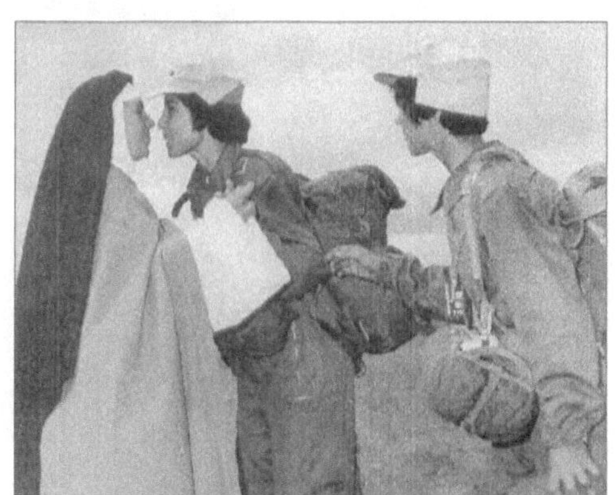

A sister from one of the nursing schools at a training jump for their former

Sister from nursing school awards berets. FAP

**Furriel Enfermeira Pára-quedista
MARIA CELESTE
FERREIRA DA COSTA**

Nasceu a 01 de Agosto de 1945, na freguesia de São João de
Tarouca, concelho de Tarouca, distrito de Lamego.

Incorporada em 26 de Agosto de 1970, como voluntária, no
Regimento de Caçadores Páraquedistas em Tancos, concluiu o Curso de
Páraquedismo e foi graduada em furriel em 09 de Outubro do mesmo ano.

Foi colocada no RCP e mais tarde no BCP 12 (Guiné em 01 de
Janeiro de 1971).

Faleceu no dia 10 de Fevereiro de 1973 na BA 12 (Guiné), quando
ia a proceder a uma evacuação, ao entrar para a aeronave foi colhida pela
hélice em movimento.

Louvada a título póstumo pelo Comandante da Zona Aérea de Cabo
Verde e Guiné, pelas suas elevadas qualidades profissionais, militares e
pessoais reveladas, em todas as evacuações em zonas de operação com
fogo inimigo, a **Furriel Graduada Enfermeira Pára-quedista FERREIRA DA
COSTA**, evidênciou notáveis qualidades de coragem, serenidade e abnegação
à causa do bem servir.

The only paranurse killed in action. B Sousa.

Books

Flight Plan Africa – Portuguese airpower in counterinsurgency. John P. Cann

Portugal's Guerrilla Wars in Africa. Al J Venter

The Chopper Boys – Helicopter Warfare in Africa. Al J Venter

Articles

A Guerra do Algodão by José Manuel Correia in Mais Alto Jan 2006

O Fiat G-91 by Tenente-General António Mimosa e Carvalho in Mais Alto 1993

Formações Aéreas Voluntárias parts 1 and 2 by Sarg. Pedro Ferreira in Mais Alto April 2004

Um Ataque Com Olhos Azuis – General (retired) José Nico.

The Imperial Airline in Revista Militar March 2012 John P Cann

O Caso dos Bombardeiros Canberra e as Relações Luso-Britânicas Durante A Guerra Colonial. José Matos Revista Militar July 2018

Os F-86 Sabre Em Combate Na Guiné. José Matos Revista Militar May 2017

Sanctuary Lost: The Air War In Portuguese Guinea, 1963 to1974. PhD dissertation of Mathew Hurley. The Ohio State University, 2009.

A Ameaça Dos Mig Na Guerra da Guiné. José Matos Revista Militar April 2015

A participação da Força Aérea Portuguesa nas guerras em África (1961-1974) – Manuel Artur Correia Alves da Costa

Various blogs by ex-combatants from all three branches of the Portuguese Armed Forces about Angola, Guinea and Mozambique and in particular:

Tabanca do Centro

http://tabancadocentro.blogspot.com

Rios dos bons sinais link (Gabriel Cavaleiro.

https://riodosbonssinais.blogspot.com/

Luís Graça & Camradas da Guiné

https://blogueforanadaevaotres.blogspot.com

www.ingramcontent.com/pod-product-compliance
Lightning Source LLC
Chambersburg PA
CBHW021400150726
47989CB00005B/2325